PRACTICAL
AWS

Cloud Solutions with Real-World Use Cases

THOMPSON CARTER

Table of Contents

CHAPTER 9: MANAGING ACCESS AND PERMISSIONS...........106

CHAPTER 10: CLOUD MONITORING AND LOGGING 116

PRACTICAL AWS: CLOUD SOLUTIONS WITH REAL-WORLD USE CASES

Why AWS is the Leading Cloud Platform

Cloud computing has redefined how businesses operate, enabling organizations to access computing resources on-demand, scale applications globally, and reduce costs. At the forefront of this transformation is Amazon Web Services (AWS), the world's leading cloud platform, trusted by millions of businesses across industries. AWS offers an unparalleled suite of services that cater to virtually every use case, from startups to enterprises, making it the backbone of the modern digital economy.

The AWS Ecosystem

AWS is not just a cloud provider; it is an ecosystem. With over 200 fully-featured services, AWS allows developers, IT professionals, and data scientists to build, deploy, and scale applications with ease. Services like Amazon EC2, S3, Lambda, and DynamoDB have become the gold standard in their respective categories. AWS's extensive global infrastructure ensures low-latency experiences for users worldwide, further cementing its position as the go-to platform for innovation.

A Game Changer for Businesses

Companies leverage AWS to launch products faster, analyze massive datasets, implement artificial intelligence, and build resilient architectures. From small startups launching their first app to global enterprises running mission-critical workloads, AWS provides the tools needed to succeed in a competitive, fast-paced world.

This book is designed to help you navigate this vast ecosystem, equipping you with practical knowledge and real-world use cases that showcase the power of AWS.

Purpose of This Book

The cloud journey can feel overwhelming, especially when confronted with the breadth of services and best practices AWS offers. Whether you're a developer, an architect, or a business leader, this book aims to:

1. **Simplify AWS Concepts**:
    - Present AWS services and solutions in a jargon-free manner.
    - Break down complex topics into digestible, actionable insights.

2. **Provide Practical Use Cases**:
    - Show real-world scenarios where AWS services solve business challenges.
    - Demonstrate how to implement these solutions step-by-step.

3. **Enable Hands-On Learning**:
    - Equip readers with examples they can replicate.
    - Encourage experimentation with AWS services to build confidence.

4. **Bridge Knowledge Gaps**:
    - Cover foundational topics for beginners while offering advanced insights for experienced users.

o Highlight emerging trends and future possibilities with AWS.

By the end of this book, you will not only understand AWS services but also know how to apply them in real-world scenarios to deliver tangible results.

Who This Book Is For

Beginners:

If you are new to AWS, this book provides a roadmap to understanding core services, deployment strategies, and best practices. From creating your first AWS account to deploying a production-grade application, this book will guide you through each step.

Intermediate Users:

For those already familiar with AWS, this book dives deeper into topics like serverless computing, hybrid cloud architectures, and advanced scaling techniques. You'll learn how to optimize costs, improve security, and build globally scalable applications.

Advanced Users and Architects:

Experienced professionals can use this book to explore cutting-edge solutions like quantum computing with Amazon Braket, multi-region replication, and advanced DevOps workflows. The focus on practical examples ensures that even complex topics are actionable.

Business Leaders:

Non-technical readers, such as product managers and business leaders, will gain insights into the capabilities of AWS. Learn how to leverage cloud solutions to achieve business goals, optimize costs, and stay ahead of the competition.

What You Will Learn

1. Foundational AWS Services

The book begins by introducing foundational AWS services like EC2 for compute, S3 for storage, and RDS for databases. These are the building blocks of any cloud solution, and mastering them is crucial for success.

2. Modern Application Architectures

From serverless computing with Lambda to container orchestration with ECS and EKS, the book covers modern approaches to building scalable, cost-efficient applications. Learn how to adopt event-driven and microservices architectures that cater to today's demands.

3. Scaling Applications Globally

AWS's global infrastructure, combined with tools like Route 53 and CloudFront, enables applications to serve users worldwide with minimal latency. The book provides step-by-step guidance on scaling applications across regions and implementing multi-region redundancy.

4. Security and Compliance

Security is a shared responsibility in the cloud, and this book highlights how to leverage AWS services like IAM, AWS WAF, and GuardDuty to secure your applications. It also explores compliance strategies for industries with stringent regulatory requirements.

5. Big Data and AI/ML

With AWS, organizations can process massive datasets and harness the power of machine learning. Learn how to use services like

Redshift, Athena, and SageMaker to turn data into actionable insights.

6. IoT and Edge Computing

As IoT and edge computing reshape industries, this book delves into how AWS IoT Core, Greengrass, and Outposts can bring these innovations to life. Real-world examples demonstrate how businesses can implement smart, low-latency solutions.

7. Cost Optimization

Effective cost management is a cornerstone of cloud success. Explore strategies to optimize AWS spending, from using reserved instances and spot instances to implementing Savings Plans and monitoring with Cost Explorer.

8. Future Trends

Prepare for the future of cloud computing with insights into emerging trends like quantum computing, green cloud practices, and serverless advancements. Discover how AWS is paving the way for innovation in these areas.

How This Book is Structured

1. Introduction and Core Concepts

The first few chapters provide a foundation in AWS, covering essential services, pricing models, and account setup. These chapters set the stage for more advanced topics.

2. Practical Use Cases

The heart of the book lies in its practical use cases. Each chapter focuses on a specific AWS solution and demonstrates how it can be applied to solve real-world problems. Examples include:

- Deploying a scalable e-commerce application.
- Building a serverless event-driven notification system.
- Implementing a disaster recovery plan for critical workloads.

3. Advanced Architectures

The latter chapters explore advanced topics like multi-region deployments, edge computing, and AI/ML integration. These chapters are designed for readers who want to push the boundaries of what AWS can do.

4. Future-Focused

The book concludes with a forward-looking perspective, discussing AWS's role in quantum computing, sustainability, and the evolving landscape of cloud technologies.

Why This Book is Unique

1. **Jargon-Free Approach**:
   - The content is designed to be accessible to readers of all technical levels.
2. **Real-World Focus**:
   - Every chapter is anchored in practical use cases, ensuring that concepts are not just theoretical but applicable.
3. **Step-by-Step Guidance**:
   - Detailed instructions and examples make it easy to follow along and replicate solutions.
4. **Future-Proofing**:
   - Covers emerging trends and prepares readers to adapt to the future of cloud computing.

Real-World Impact

Empowering Startups

Startups can use this book to build scalable architectures that grow with their business. By leveraging AWS's pay-as-you-go model, startups can innovate without incurring significant upfront costs.

Optimizing Enterprises

Enterprises with existing cloud deployments can refine their strategies using the book's cost optimization tips, multi-region replication techniques, and hybrid cloud solutions.

Enabling Innovation

Developers and architects can push boundaries by exploring advanced topics like AI/ML integration, IoT, and edge computing. The examples in this book demonstrate how AWS accelerates innovation across industries.

A Call to Action

The cloud is not just a technology—it's a mindset. AWS empowers individuals and organizations to reimagine what's possible, and this book is your guide to unlocking that potential. Whether you're building your first application or architecting solutions for millions of users, the knowledge in this book will help you succeed.

Let's embark on this journey together. By the end of this book, you'll not only understand AWS but also feel confident applying its services to create solutions that make a real-world impact. Let's build the future with AWS.

CHAPTER 1: INTRODUCTION TO AWS

Amazon Web Services (AWS) has revolutionized the way businesses deploy, manage, and scale their applications. As the leading cloud platform, AWS offers an extensive range of services to support enterprises, startups, and individual developers. This chapter provides an overview of what AWS is, its benefits, and its service categories, along with a real-world example of how a small business can leverage AWS to transform its operations.

What is AWS, and Why is it the Leading Cloud Platform?

What is AWS?

Amazon Web Services (AWS) is a comprehensive cloud computing platform developed by Amazon. It provides on-demand access to a wide array of computing resources, including servers, storage, databases, networking, artificial intelligence (AI), and machine learning (ML). AWS operates on a pay-as-you-go model, allowing users to pay only for the resources they use.

Why AWS Leads the Cloud Market

AWS dominates the cloud computing industry for several reasons:

1. **Early Market Entry**:
   - Launched in 2006, AWS was one of the first cloud providers, giving it a significant head start in developing and refining its services.

2. **Comprehensive Service Offering**:
   - AWS offers over **200 services** across compute, storage, databases, networking, machine learning, analytics, and more. This breadth allows customers to find solutions for nearly any use case.

3. **Global Infrastructure**:
   - AWS has a vast global network of **data centers**, called Availability Zones and Regions, ensuring high availability and low latency.

4. **Continuous Innovation**:
   - AWS consistently adds new features, services, and enhancements, staying ahead of competitors.

5. **Strong Ecosystem**:

- o AWS integrates seamlessly with a wide range of third-party tools and technologies, making it adaptable to diverse environments.

Key Benefits of Cloud Computing with AWS

1. Cost Efficiency

- Traditional IT setups require upfront investments in hardware and maintenance. AWS eliminates these costs by offering on-demand services.
- Pricing models include **pay-as-you-go**, **Savings Plans**, and **reserved instances**, enabling businesses to optimize costs.

2. Scalability and Elasticity

- With AWS, businesses can scale their infrastructure up or down based on demand, ensuring they only use (and pay for) the resources they need.
- For example, during peak traffic, an e-commerce site can automatically provision additional servers to handle the load.

3. Reliability

- AWS is built on a global infrastructure with multiple data centers. Features like **Auto Scaling**, **Elastic Load Balancing**, and **multi-region deployments** ensure reliability and fault tolerance.

4. Security

- AWS follows a **shared responsibility model**, offering robust security measures like encryption, firewalls, and identity management tools.
- Services like **IAM (Identity and Access Management)** and **AWS Shield** help businesses protect sensitive data.

5. Innovation and Speed

- AWS enables rapid experimentation and deployment. Developers can test new features, deploy updates, and launch products faster.

6. Access to Advanced Technologies

- AWS democratizes access to cutting-edge technologies like **machine learning**, **big data analytics**, and **IoT**, making them accessible to businesses of all sizes.

Overview of AWS Services and Categories

AWS offers a vast array of services across several categories. Here's a high-level overview of some of the most important ones:

1. Compute

- **Amazon EC2 (Elastic Compute Cloud)**: Virtual servers for hosting applications.
- **AWS Lambda**: Serverless computing for running code without managing infrastructure.
- **Amazon ECS/EKS**: Managed services for containerized applications.

2. Storage

- **Amazon S3 (Simple Storage Service)**: Object storage for data of any size.

- **Amazon EBS (Elastic Block Store)**: Storage for use with EC2 instances.
- **Amazon Glacier**: Archival storage for long-term data retention.

3. Databases

- **Amazon RDS (Relational Database Service)**: Managed relational databases (e.g., MySQL, PostgreSQL, SQL Server).
- **Amazon DynamoDB**: Managed NoSQL database for high-performance applications.
- **Amazon Redshift**: Data warehouse for analytics.

4. Networking

- **Amazon VPC (Virtual Private Cloud)**: Isolated network environments.
- **Elastic Load Balancing (ELB)**: Distributes traffic across servers.
- **Amazon Route 53**: Domain name system (DNS) and traffic management.

5. Machine Learning and AI

- **Amazon SageMaker**: Build, train, and deploy machine learning models.
- **Amazon Rekognition**: Image and video analysis.
- **Amazon Polly**: Text-to-speech conversion.

6. Analytics

- **Amazon Athena**: Query data in S3 using SQL.
- **AWS Glue**: Managed ETL (Extract, Transform, Load) service.
- **Amazon EMR**: Big data processing with Hadoop and Spark.

7. Developer Tools

- **AWS CodePipeline**: Continuous integration and deployment.
- **AWS CloudFormation**: Infrastructure as code (IaC) service.
- **AWS SDKs and CLI**: Programmatic access to AWS.

8. Security and Identity

- **IAM (Identity and Access Management)**: Manage user permissions.
- **AWS WAF (Web Application Firewall)**: Protect web applications from attacks.
- **AWS Shield**: DDoS protection service.

Real-World Example: A Small Business Migrating to AWS

Scenario

A local retail business with an outdated on-premises IT setup wants to:

1. Reduce maintenance costs.
2. Improve website reliability during peak traffic (e.g., holiday sales).
3. Implement a secure and scalable solution for managing customer data.

Solution

1. **Compute**:
   - Use **Amazon EC2** to host their website and enable Auto Scaling to handle spikes in traffic.

2. **Storage**:
   - o Store product images and customer records on **Amazon S3**, ensuring durability and availability.
3. **Database**:
   - o Use **Amazon RDS** (MySQL) to manage customer orders and inventory.
4. **Security**:
   - o Implement **IAM** to control access, ensuring only authorized employees can modify resources.
5. **Cost Optimization**:
   - o Use the **Savings Plan** pricing model to reduce costs for consistently running EC2 instances.

Outcome

- The business reduces infrastructure costs by 40%.
- Website reliability improves with minimal downtime during peak hours.
- Customer data is secured, meeting regulatory compliance requirements.

This chapter has introduced AWS, its benefits, and its diverse service offerings. You've learned why AWS is the leading cloud platform and explored how it can transform businesses of all sizes. Moving forward, we'll delve deeper into AWS's individual services and demonstrate how to implement them for practical use cases.

CHAPTER 2: SETTING UP YOUR AWS ACCOUNT

Setting up an AWS account is the first step toward leveraging the power of cloud computing. In this chapter, you'll learn how to create an AWS account, navigate the AWS Management Console, and implement best practices to secure your account. Additionally, we'll explore a real-world example of setting up an account for a small software company.

Step-by-Step Guide to Creating an AWS Account

1. Access the AWS Signup Page

- Visit the AWS Signup page.
- Click on the **"Create an AWS Account"** button.

2. Enter Account Details

You'll need to provide:

- **Email Address**: This will be the root user for your account.
- **Account Name**: Choose a name for your AWS account (e.g., "XYZ Software Solutions").
- **Password**: Create a strong password.

3. Select an AWS Support Plan

AWS offers four support plans:

1. **Basic (Free)**: Ideal for learning and small-scale use.
2. **Developer**: For experimenting with support from AWS.
3. **Business**: For mission-critical workloads.
4. **Enterprise**: For large-scale enterprise needs.

Choose the plan that fits your requirements. Most users start with the **Basic plan**.

4. Provide Payment Information

- Enter a valid credit or debit card for billing purposes.
- AWS will perform a small charge (usually $1) to verify your card, which will be refunded shortly.

5. Confirm Your Identity

- Enter a valid phone number.
- Complete the automated verification process by entering the code sent to your phone.

6. Customize Your Account

- After verification, sign in to the AWS Management Console.
- You'll have access to the **AWS Free Tier**, which provides free usage for many services (e.g., 750 hours of EC2 per month for 12 months).

Navigating the AWS Management Console

The **AWS Management Console** is your control center for managing AWS services. Here's a quick guide to its key components:

1. Dashboard

The console opens to the **AWS Management Console Home**. From here, you can:

- Search for services using the search bar at the top.
- Access **Recently Visited Services** for quick navigation.
- View tutorials and AWS resources.

2. Service Categories

On the navigation bar:

- Click on **Services** to view a categorized list of all AWS services (e.g., Compute, Storage, Networking).
- Example: To launch a virtual machine, click **Compute > EC2**.

3. Global Settings

On the top-right corner:

- **Region Selection**: Choose a geographic region for your services (e.g., US East (N. Virginia), Europe (Frankfurt)).
    - Use the region closest to your target audience for lower latency.
- **Account Dropdown**: Manage account settings, billing, and security credentials.

4. Resource Management

Access a comprehensive overview of your resources through:

- **AWS Resource Groups**: View and organize resources by tags.
- **Billing Dashboard**: Monitor costs, usage, and Free Tier balance.

5. AWS Marketplace

The **AWS Marketplace** is a catalog of third-party software, services, and solutions. You can:

- Find pre-configured AMIs (Amazon Machine Images).
- Purchase SaaS solutions for easy integration.

Best Practices for Account Security

Securing your AWS account is critical to prevent unauthorized access and data breaches. Follow these best practices to ensure your account remains secure:

1. Enable Multi-Factor Authentication (MFA)

MFA adds an extra layer of security by requiring a one-time code from your phone or hardware token.

Steps to Enable MFA:

1. Go to **IAM > Security Credentials > MFA**.
2. Select **Manage MFA** and follow the instructions to link an authenticator app like Google Authenticator or Authy.

2. Create IAM Users

Avoid using the root user for day to-day tasks. Instead:

- Create individual **IAM users** for each team member.
- Assign permissions based on their roles (e.g., Developer, Admin).

Example:

- A developer working on EC2 should have permissions for only EC2-related tasks.

3. Use Billing Alerts

Set up billing alerts to monitor costs and avoid unexpected charges:

1. Go to **Billing > Billing Preferences**.
2. Enable **Receive Billing Alerts**.
3. Use **CloudWatch Billing Alarms** to receive notifications when costs exceed a threshold.

4. Secure API Access

For programmatic access to AWS:

- Generate **Access Keys** via the IAM console.
- Store keys securely using tools like AWS Secrets Manager or environment variables.
- Rotate keys periodically and disable unused ones.

5. Monitor Account Activity

Use AWS CloudTrail to track and log all account activities, including API calls and console logins. This helps detect unauthorized access.

Real-World Example: Setting Up an Account for a Small Software Company

Scenario

XYZ Software Solutions is a small company building a SaaS product. They plan to migrate their existing application infrastructure to AWS for better scalability and cost management. Here's how they set up their AWS account:

Steps

1. **Create the Account**:
   - The CTO creates the AWS account using the company email.
   - They opt for the **Basic Support Plan**.

2. **Secure the Account**:
   - The root user is protected with MFA.
   - Individual IAM users are created for developers, each with permissions for specific AWS services (e.g., EC2, RDS).

3. **Set Up Billing Alerts**:

- A CloudWatch Billing Alarm is configured to notify the finance team if monthly costs exceed $500.

4. **Organize Resources**:
   - Tags are applied to all resources (e.g., Environment=Production, Team=DevOps) to simplify cost tracking and resource grouping.

5. **Select the Region**:
   - Since most of their customers are in North America, they choose **US East (N. Virginia)** as their primary region.

6. **Use the Free Tier**:
   - Developers start by using Free Tier resources, such as:
     - 750 hours of EC2 t2.micro instances.
     - 5 GB of S3 storage for testing static content delivery.

Outcome

Within a week, XYZ Software Solutions sets up their account securely, provisions test environments, and begins their AWS migration journey without incurring unnecessary costs.

Setting up an AWS account is a straightforward process, but implementing best practices for security and cost management is essential. In this chapter, you learned how to:

- Create and configure an AWS account.
- Navigate the AWS Management Console.
- Secure your account using IAM, MFA, and billing alerts.
- Apply these concepts in a real-world scenario for a small business.

With your AWS account ready, it's time to dive into the core services, starting with **compute resources in Chapter 3**. Let's build your first cloud infrastructure

CHAPTER 3: CORE COMPUTE SERVICES

AWS compute services form the backbone of cloud-based applications, enabling you to run virtual machines, containers, and serverless functions. This chapter focuses on one of the most widely used AWS compute services: **Amazon Elastic Compute Cloud (EC2)**. You'll learn how to create and manage virtual machines, explore EC2 instance types and pricing, and implement scaling strategies. We'll conclude with a real-world example of hosting a website on EC2.

Introduction to EC2 (Elastic Compute Cloud)

What is EC2?

Amazon EC2 is a cloud-based virtual server that lets you run applications without managing physical hardware. With EC2, you can:

- Launch and terminate servers on demand.
- Customize compute power, memory, storage, and networking.
- Choose pre-configured machine images or create your own.

Why Use EC2?

- **Scalability**: Easily scale resources to handle changes in demand.
- **Flexibility**: Choose from a wide range of operating systems (Linux, Windows) and configurations.
- **Cost-Effective**: Pay only for the compute time you use.
- **Global Availability**: Deploy applications closer to users using AWS regions.

Creating and Managing Virtual Machines

Step 1: Launch an EC2 Instance

1. **Sign in to the AWS Management Console**:
   - o Navigate to **EC2** under the **Compute** category.
2. **Choose an Amazon Machine Image (AMI)**:
   - o Select a pre-configured AMI (e.g., Amazon Linux, Ubuntu, or Windows Server).
   - o Example: Choose **Amazon Linux 2 AMI** for a basic Linux server.
3. **Choose an Instance Type**:
   - o Pick an instance type based on your application's needs (e.g., t2.micro for low-cost general use).
4. **Configure Instance Details**:
   - o Define the instance count, network settings (VPC, subnet), and IAM roles.
5. **Add Storage**:
   - o Attach storage volumes. The default root volume is often sufficient for basic use.
6. **Configure Security Groups**:
   - o Create or select a security group to define inbound and outbound rules.
   - o Example: Allow inbound HTTP (port 80) and SSH (port 22) traffic.

7. **Launch the Instance**:

   o   Review and confirm your configuration.

   o   Generate and download a key pair (.pem file) for SSH access.

Step 2: Connect to Your EC2 Instance

1. Use the **Public IP Address** of the EC2 instance.
2. Connect via SSH:

bash

ssh -i your-key.pem ec2-user@your-ec2-public-ip

Replace your-key.pem with the path to your key file and your-ec2-public-ip with the instance's public IP.

Step 3: Install and Run Applications

• Update the instance:

bash

```
sudo yum update -y
```

- Install a web server (e.g., Apache):

```bash
bash

sudo yum install httpd -y
sudo systemctl start httpd
sudo systemctl enable httpd
```

- Place your website files in /var/www/html/.

Step 4: Monitor and Manage Instances

Use the EC2 Dashboard to:

- View running instances.
- Stop, start, or terminate instances.
- Monitor performance metrics like CPU usage and network traffic.

EC2 Instance Types, Pricing, and Scaling

Instance Types

EC2 offers various instance families optimized for specific workloads:

1. **General Purpose**:
   - o   Balanced compute, memory, and storage.
   - o   Example: t2.micro, t3.medium.
   - o   Use Case: Web servers, small databases.

2. **Compute Optimized**:
   - o   High-performance processors.
   - o   Example: c5.large, c6g.xlarge.
   - o   Use Case: High-performance computing, gaming.

3. **Memory Optimized**:
   - o   High memory for memory-intensive applications.
   - o   Example: r5.large, x1e.xlarge.
   - o   Use Case: In-memory databases, big data processing.

4. **Storage Optimized**:
   - o   High-speed local storage for large datasets.
   - o   Example: i3.large, d2.xlarge.
   - o   Use Case: Data warehousing, distributed storage.

5. **GPU Instances**:

- o Optimized for machine learning and graphics rendering.
- o Example: p3.2xlarge, g4dn.xlarge.

Pricing Models

1. **On-Demand**:
   - o Pay for compute capacity by the second.
   - o Ideal for short-term workloads or testing.
2. **Reserved Instances**:
   - o Commit to a 1- or 3-year term for lower pricing.
   - o Best for predictable, long-term usage.
3. **Spot Instances**:
   - o Use spare EC2 capacity at a steep discount.
   - o Suitable for batch jobs or fault-tolerant applications.
4. **Savings Plans**:
   - o Flexible pricing for long-term commitments across instance families.

Scaling with EC2

1. **Manual Scaling**:

- Manually launch or terminate instances based on demand.

2. **Auto Scaling**:
   - Define scaling policies to add/remove instances automatically.
   - Example: Scale up during traffic spikes and scale down during low usage.

3. **Elastic Load Balancing (ELB)**:
   - Distribute traffic across multiple instances for better performance and fault tolerance.

Real-World Example: Hosting a Website Using EC2 Instances

Scenario

A small software company wants to host their corporate website using AWS. The website must handle occasional traffic spikes during product launches while keeping costs low.

Solution

1. **Launch EC2 Instance**:
   - Use the **Amazon Linux 2 AMI** with a t2.micro instance for low-cost hosting.

o Configure inbound rules to allow HTTP and SSH access.

2. **Install Web Server**:

   o Install Apache and upload the website files to /var/www/html.

3. **Add a Domain Name**:

   o Use **Route 53** to configure a custom domain (e.g., www.xyzsoftware.com) and point it to the EC2 instance's public IP.

4. **Enable Auto Scaling**:

   o Set up an Auto Scaling group with policies to add instances during high traffic periods (e.g., product launches) and terminate them during off-peak hours.

5. **Monitor and Optimize**:

   o Use **CloudWatch** to monitor CPU usage and ensure the instance is performing well.

   o Set up alerts to notify the team if usage exceeds thresholds.

Outcome

- The company successfully hosts their website with minimal upfront costs.
- Auto Scaling ensures the site remains responsive during traffic spikes without incurring unnecessary expenses during low usage periods.
- The team focuses on enhancing the website's content while AWS handles infrastructure reliability.

In this chapter, we introduced Amazon EC2 as a cornerstone of AWS's compute services. You learned how to create and manage virtual machines, explored instance types and pricing models, and implemented scaling strategies. The real-world example demonstrated how a small business can use EC2 to host a reliable and scalable website.

In the next chapter, we'll explore **Serverless Computing with AWS Lambda**, where you can run code without managing servers. Let's continue building on this foundation!

CHAPTER 4: SERVERLESS COMPUTING WITH AWS LAMBDA

Serverless computing is a paradigm shift in cloud architecture, enabling developers to build and run applications without managing servers. AWS Lambda, a cornerstone of serverless computing on AWS, lets you execute code in response to events without worrying about provisioning or maintaining infrastructure. In this chapter, you'll explore what serverless computing is, learn to create and deploy Lambda functions, integrate them with other AWS services, and implement a real-world event-driven image processing workflow.

What is Serverless Computing?

Definition

Serverless computing allows developers to focus solely on writing code, while the cloud provider handles infrastructure management. In a serverless model:

- Servers are still used but abstracted away from the developer.
- Resources are automatically scaled based on demand.

- You only pay for the compute time used.

Key Features

1. **Event-Driven**:
   - Functions are triggered by events, such as file uploads or HTTP requests.
2. **Auto-Scaling**:
   - Automatically scales up or down based on the workload.
3. **Pay-As-You-Go**:
   - Charges are based on the number of requests and compute time, measured in milliseconds.
4. **No Infrastructure Management**:
   - Developers don't need to manage servers, operating systems, or scaling policies.

Why Use Serverless Computing?

- **Cost Efficiency**: No charges when the function isn't running.
- **Agility**: Faster development and deployment cycles.
- **Scalability**: Handles spikes in demand seamlessly.

- **Focus on Code**: Developers can focus on application logic, not infrastructure.

Creating and Deploying Lambda Functions

Step 1: Create a Lambda Function

1. **Sign in to AWS Management Console.**
2. Navigate to **AWS Lambda** and click **Create Function**.
3. Choose **Author from scratch**:
   - **Function name**: imageProcessor
   - **Runtime**: Select a runtime (e.g., Python 3.9 or Node.js).
4. Set up **Execution Role**:
   - Use an existing role or create a new one with permissions to access required AWS services (e.g., S3).

Step 2: Write Function Code

Write code directly in the AWS Lambda console or upload a ZIP file containing your code and dependencies.

Example (Python):

python

```python
import boto3

def lambda_handler(event, context):
    # Log the event
    print("Event:", event)

    # Example logic: Access an S3 bucket
    s3 = boto3.client('s3')
    bucket_name = event['Records'][0]['s3']['bucket']['name']
    object_key = event['Records'][0]['s3']['object']['key']

    print(f"File uploaded: {object_key} in bucket: {bucket_name}")
    return {"statusCode": 200, "body": "File processed successfully"}
```

Step 3: Configure the Trigger

1. Select a trigger for your Lambda function:

o   Example: S3 trigger for file uploads.

2. Configure the trigger source:

o   Specify the S3 bucket and event type (e.g., PUT for uploads).

Step 4: Test and Deploy

1. Test the function using the built-in test utility.

o   Provide a test event in JSON format.

2. Deploy the function and make it live.

Example Test Event (S3):

json

```
{
  "Records": [
    {
      "s3": {
        "bucket": {
          "name": "my-test-bucket"
        },
        "object": {
```

```
      "key": "example-image.jpg"
    }
   }
  }
 ]
}
```

Integrating Lambda with Other AWS Services

AWS Lambda is designed to integrate seamlessly with other AWS services, enabling complex workflows. Common integrations include:

1. S3 (Simple Storage Service)

- Trigger a Lambda function when a file is uploaded to an S3 bucket.
- Example: Resize an image or process a CSV file.

2. DynamoDB

- Use Lambda to process real-time updates in DynamoDB streams.

- Example: Analyze new records added to a database.

3. API Gateway

- Expose Lambda functions as RESTful APIs using Amazon API Gateway.
- Example: Create a serverless backend for a web or mobile app.

4. Step Functions

- Orchestrate complex workflows by chaining multiple Lambda functions.
- Example: Multi-step data processing pipeline.

5. EventBridge

- Respond to custom events from applications or AWS services.
- Example: Trigger Lambda to notify admins when certain thresholds are met.

Real-World Example: Building an Event-Driven Image Processing Workflow

Scenario

A company needs to automate the processing of images uploaded to an S3 bucket. Uploaded images should be resized to multiple dimensions for use in a web application.

Solution

Using AWS Lambda, S3, and CloudWatch, the workflow automates image processing:

1. **S3 Trigger**:
   o An image upload to the original-images bucket triggers the Lambda function.
2. **Lambda Function**:
   o Resizes the image to predefined dimensions (e.g., thumbnails and banners).
   o Stores the resized images in the processed-images bucket.
3. **CloudWatch Logs**:

o Logs all processing events for monitoring and debugging.

Implementation Steps

1. Set Up the S3 Buckets

- Create two buckets:
    - o original-images for uploads.
    - o processed-images for resized images.

2. Create the Lambda Function Write a Python Lambda function to resize images:

python

```python
import boto3
from PIL import Image
import io

s3 = boto3.client('s3')

def resize_image(image_data, size):
    img = Image.open(io.BytesIO(image_data))
```

```python
        img.thumbnail(size)
        buffer = io.BytesIO()
        img.save(buffer, "JPEG")
        buffer.seek(0)
        return buffer

def lambda_handler(event, context):
    bucket_name = event['Records'][0]['s3']['bucket']['name']
    object_key = event['Records'][0]['s3']['object']['key']

    # Download the image
    response          =          s3.get_object(Bucket=bucket_name,
Key=object_key)
    image_data = response['Body'].read()

    # Resize the image
    sizes = {"thumbnail": (100, 100), "banner": (800, 200)}
    for name, size in sizes.items():
        resized_image = resize_image(image_data, size)
        new_key = f"{name}/{object_key}"
```

```
s3.put_object(Bucket="processed-images",    Key=new_key,
Body=resized_image, ContentType="image/jpeg")


return  {"statusCode": 200, "body": f"Image {object_key}
processed successfully."}
```

3. Configure the S3 Trigger

- Set the original-images bucket to trigger the Lambda function on PUT events.

4. Test the Workflow

- Upload an image to the original-images bucket and verify that resized images appear in the processed-images bucket.

Outcome

- The company automates image resizing without provisioning or managing servers.
- Resized images are organized by size (thumbnail/, banner/) in the processed-images bucket.
- CloudWatch logs provide insights into function execution and performance.

AWS Lambda empowers developers to build scalable, event-driven applications without managing infrastructure. In this chapter, you learned:

1. What serverless computing is and why it's useful.
2. How to create and deploy Lambda functions.
3. How to integrate Lambda with services like S3, API Gateway, and DynamoDB.
4. A real-world example of using Lambda for image processing.

In the next chapter, we'll dive into **Storage Basics with Amazon S3**, where you'll learn how to store, retrieve, and manage data efficiently in the cloud. Let's continue building!

CHAPTER 5: STORAGE BASICS WITH AMAZON S3

Amazon S3 (Simple Storage Service) is one of the most widely used storage services in the cloud. It is designed for scalability, durability, and flexibility, making it ideal for storing everything from simple text files to large multimedia assets. In this chapter, you'll learn the basics of S3, how to store and retrieve data, implement security and management features, and use S3 for a practical real-world example: hosting static website content.

Introduction to Amazon S3

What is Amazon S3?

Amazon S3 is an object storage service that enables you to store, retrieve, and manage data in the cloud. Key characteristics of S3 include:

- **Object-Based Storage**: Data is stored as objects within buckets.
- **Unlimited Scalability**: Store as much data as needed.

- **High Durability**: Designed for 99.999999999% (11 nines) durability.
- **Global Accessibility**: Access data from anywhere via HTTPS.

Key Concepts

1. **Buckets**:
   - o Containers for storing objects (files).
   - o Each bucket must have a globally unique name.
   - o Example: my-awesome-website-bucket.
2. **Objects**:
   - o Individual files stored in S3.
   - o Each object is identified by a unique **key** (name).
3. **Data Consistency**:
   - o S3 provides strong consistency for read-after-write operations.
4. **Storage Classes**:
   - o Choose a class based on data access patterns:
     - ▪ **Standard**: General-purpose, frequently accessed data.

- **Intelligent-Tiering**: Automatically moves data to cost-effective storage tiers.
- **Glacier**: Archival storage for infrequently accessed data.

Storing, Retrieving, and Managing Data in S3 Buckets

Step 1: Create a Bucket

1. Go to the **S3 Dashboard** in the AWS Management Console.
2. Click **Create Bucket**.
3. Configure the bucket:
   - **Bucket Name**: Choose a unique name (e.g., my-static-website).
   - **Region**: Select the closest AWS Region for lower latency.
   - **Public Access**: Decide whether to block or allow public access (useful for static websites).

Step 2: Upload Objects

1. Open the bucket and click **Upload**.
2. Drag and drop files or browse to select files.

3. Set permissions for each file (e.g., public or private access).

4. Click **Upload**.

Step 3: Retrieve Objects

- **Console**:
  - ○ Click the file in the bucket to get its **Object URL**.
  - ○ Example URL: https://my-static-website.s3.amazonaws.com/image.jpg.
- **Command Line (AWS CLI)**:

bash

```
aws s3 cp s3://my-static-website/image.jpg ./downloaded-image.jpg
```

- **SDK (Python Example)**:

python

```
import boto3

s3 = boto3.client('s3')
```

```
s3.download_file('my-static-website',          'image.jpg',
'downloaded-image.jpg')
```

Step 4: Manage Data

1. **Delete Objects**:
   - o In the console, select the file and click **Delete**.
   - o Or use the AWS CLI:

   bash

   ```
   aws s3 rm s3://my-static-website/image.jpg
   ```

2. **Organize Files with Folders**:
   - o S3 uses a flat structure but allows pseudo-folders by using prefixes in object keys (e.g., folder1/image.jpg).

Security, Versioning, and Lifecycle Policies

1. Security

- **Access Control**:
  - Use **IAM Roles** to control who can access S3 buckets and objects.
  - For public access, update bucket policies carefully to prevent unintended exposure.
- **Encryption**:
  - Enable **S3 Default Encryption** to encrypt data at rest using:
    - **SSE-S3** (S3-managed keys).
    - **SSE-KMS** (AWS Key Management Service).
  - Example Policy:

  json

```json
{
  "Version": "2012-10-17",
  "Statement": [
    {
      "Effect": "Allow",
      "Principal": "*",
      "Action": "s3:GetObject",
```

```
        "Resource": "arn:aws:s3:::my-static-website/*"
    }
  ]
}
```

2. Versioning

- **What It Does**:
  - o Tracks multiple versions of objects.
  - o Protects against accidental deletions or overwrites.
- **How to Enable**:
  - o Go to the bucket's **Properties** tab.
  - o Enable **Bucket Versioning**.
- **Access Object Versions**:
  - o Use the AWS CLI:

    bash

    aws s3api list-object-versions --bucket my-static-website

3. Lifecycle Policies

- **Purpose**:
    - Automate transitions to cost-effective storage classes or delete old data.
- **How to Set Up**:
    - Open the bucket's **Management** tab.
    - Create a **Lifecycle Rule**:
        - Example: Transition objects to Glacier after 30 days and delete after 365 days.

Real-World Example: Hosting Static Website Content on S3

Scenario

A small business wants to host its company website, consisting of static HTML, CSS, and JavaScript files. They require a simple, scalable, and low-cost solution.

Solution

Use Amazon S3 to host the static website. Follow these steps:

Step 1: Create a Bucket

1. Name the bucket (e.g., my-company-website).
2. Allow public access for website hosting.

Step 2: Upload Website Files

1. Upload all static files (e.g., index.html, style.css, and images) to the bucket.
2. Ensure files like index.html are publicly accessible.

Step 3: Configure Bucket for Website Hosting

1. Go to the **Properties** tab of the bucket.
2. Enable **Static Website Hosting**:
   - Specify the index document (index.html).
   - Optionally, specify an error document (error.html).

Step 4: Get the Website URL

1. S3 provides a public endpoint for the website:
   - Example: http://my-company-website.s3-website-us-east-1.amazonaws.com.

Step 5: (Optional) Use a Custom Domain

1. Use **Route 53** or another DNS provider to map your domain to the S3 bucket.

2. Configure an **Alias Record** for the domain.

Outcome

- The website is hosted and accessible via the S3 bucket URL or custom domain.
- The business benefits from:
  - High scalability.
  - Minimal costs (S3 pricing for storage and bandwidth).
  - Simple deployment by uploading files directly.

Amazon S3 is a versatile storage service suitable for a wide range of use cases. In this chapter, you learned:

1. The fundamentals of Amazon S3, including buckets and objects.
2. How to store, retrieve, and manage data.
3. Important security measures like encryption and access control.
4. Practical features like versioning and lifecycle policies.

5. A real-world example of hosting static websites using S3.

In the next chapter, we'll dive into **Databases on AWS**, exploring how to manage relational and NoSQL databases in the cloud. Let's keep building!

CHAPTER 6: DATABASES ON AWS

AWS offers a range of managed database services that cater to a variety of application needs, from traditional relational databases to modern NoSQL solutions. This chapter provides an overview of relational and NoSQL databases, introduces Amazon RDS and DynamoDB, and offers guidance on choosing the right database for your application. We'll conclude with a real-world example of scaling a social media app database.

Overview of Relational and NoSQL Databases

1. Relational Databases

Relational databases store data in structured tables with rows and columns. They rely on schemas and support SQL (Structured Query Language) for querying and managing data.

Key Features:

- Schema-based design.
- ACID (Atomicity, Consistency, Isolation, Durability) compliance for reliable transactions.
- Strong relationships through **primary** and **foreign keys**.

Common Use Cases:

- E-commerce platforms (product and user data).
- Financial applications (transaction processing).

Examples:

- MySQL, PostgreSQL, Microsoft SQL Server, Oracle Database.

2. NoSQL Databases

NoSQL databases are designed for unstructured or semi-structured data and prioritize scalability and flexibility. Types of NoSQL databases include:

- **Key-Value Stores**: Simple key-value pairs (e.g., DynamoDB).
- **Document Stores**: JSON-like documents (e.g., MongoDB).
- **Column-Family Stores**: Optimized for large-scale analytics (e.g., Cassandra).
- **Graph Databases**: Focus on relationships (e.g., Neo4j).

Key Features:

- Schema-less design for flexibility.
- Horizontal scaling for high traffic and large datasets.
- Optimized for specific use cases (e.g., caching, real-time analytics).

Common Use Cases:

- Social media applications (user profiles, activity feeds).
- IoT and mobile apps (real-time data ingestion).

Introduction to Amazon RDS and DynamoDB

Amazon RDS (Relational Database Service)

Amazon RDS is a managed service for relational databases. It simplifies setup, scaling, and maintenance tasks like backups, updates, and monitoring.

Supported Engines:

- MySQL
- PostgreSQL
- MariaDB
- Oracle
- Microsoft SQL Server
- Amazon Aurora (AWS's high-performance relational database).

Key Features:

1. **Fully Managed**:
   - Handles backups, software patching, and failover automatically.
2. **Scalability**:

    o   Supports read replicas and storage scaling.

3. **Performance Optimization**:

    o   Amazon Aurora provides up to 5x the performance of standard MySQL.

4. **High Availability**:

    o   Multi-AZ (Availability Zone) deployments for fault tolerance.

Getting Started with RDS:

1. Go to the **RDS Dashboard**.
2. Create a database instance by selecting an engine (e.g., MySQL).
3. Configure settings like storage size, instance type, and multi-AZ replication.
4. Connect to the database using standard SQL clients.

Amazon DynamoDB

DynamoDB is a NoSQL database designed for low-latency, high-throughput applications. It is fully managed and scales automatically to handle millions of requests per second.

Key Features:

1. **Key-Value and Document Store**:
   o   Store JSON-like documents or key-value pairs.
2. **Serverless**:
   o   No need to manage infrastructure; AWS handles scaling.
3. **High Availability**:
   o   Data is replicated across multiple Availability Zones.
4. **Global Tables**:
   o   Multi-region replication for global applications.

Getting Started with DynamoDB:

1. Go to the **DynamoDB Dashboard**.
2. Create a table by specifying a primary key (partition key and optional sort key).
3. Insert data using the console, AWS CLI, or SDKs.

4. Query and scan the table using the API or AWS CLI.

Choosing the Right Database for Your Application

When to Use RDS:

- **Structured Data**: Data fits well into rows and columns with defined relationships.
- **Transaction Requirements**: Applications requiring ACID compliance.
- **Standardized Queries**: Heavy use of SQL for data manipulation.
- **Examples**:
  - o Inventory management systems.
  - o Financial transaction processing.

When to Use DynamoDB:

- **Unstructured or Semi-Structured Data**: Flexible schema-less design.
- **High Traffic Applications**: Applications requiring low-latency performance at scale.

- **Simple Data Models**: Use cases with straightforward key-value or document structures.
- **Examples**:
    - Real-time leaderboards.
    - IoT sensor data collection.

Comparison: RDS vs. DynamoDB

Feature	Amazon RDS	Amazon DynamoDB
Data Model	Relational (structured)	Key-Value, Document
Scalability	Vertical and Read Replicas	Horizontal, Serverless
Latency	Milliseconds	Microseconds
Use Case	Complex relationships, ACID	High traffic, low latency apps
Examples	E-commerce, financial apps	Social media, IoT, gaming apps

Real-World Example: Scaling a Social Media App Database

Scenario

A startup launches a social media app where users can:

1. Create profiles and upload posts.
2. View activity feeds in real time.
3. Interact with posts through likes and comments.

The app requires:

- A relational database for structured user data and relationships.
- A NoSQL database for fast and scalable activity feed storage.

Solution

1. **User Profiles with Amazon RDS**:
   o **Database**: Amazon Aurora (MySQL-compatible).
   o **Schema**:
      ▪ **Users Table**: Stores user information (name, email, profile picture).

- **Relationships Table**: Manages friend/follower connections.
  - **Benefits**:
    - Structured queries for retrieving user details.
    - ACID compliance ensures data consistency.

2. **Activity Feeds with DynamoDB**:
   - **Table Design**:
     - Partition Key: user_id.
     - Sort Key: timestamp.
     - Attributes: post_id, content, likes, comments.
   - **Benefits**:
     - High write throughput for real-time post creation.
     - Low-latency reads for fetching feeds.

3. **Integration**:
   - User data from RDS is used to display profile details.
   - Activity feeds are fetched from DynamoDB for fast performance.

Outcome

- The app handles rapid growth with scalable and efficient databases.
- User profiles are consistent and reliable due to RDS's ACID compliance.
- DynamoDB ensures real-time performance for activity feeds, even during traffic spikes.

Databases are critical components of modern applications, and AWS offers a range of solutions to meet diverse requirements. In this chapter, you learned:

1. The differences between relational and NoSQL databases.
2. The features and use cases of Amazon RDS and DynamoDB.
3. How to choose the right database based on application needs.
4. A real-world example of using RDS and DynamoDB to scale a social media app.

In the next chapter, we'll dive into **Networking Essentials**, exploring how AWS enables secure and scalable networking for cloud applications. Let's keep building!

CHAPTER 7: NETWORKING ESSENTIALS

Networking is the backbone of any cloud infrastructure. Amazon Web Services (AWS) provides a robust and flexible networking solution called the **Virtual Private Cloud (VPC)**, allowing you to create secure and scalable networks tailored to your applications. This chapter introduces the basics of VPC, including subnets, route tables, and security groups. You'll also learn how to set up secure, scalable architectures and deploy a multi-region application in a real-world example.

Basics of VPC (Virtual Private Cloud)

What is a VPC?

A **Virtual Private Cloud (VPC)** is a logically isolated network in AWS where you can define your own IP address ranges, subnets, route tables, and security configurations. It's your private space in the AWS cloud, allowing you to control how your resources communicate internally and externally.

Key Features of a VPC

1. **Customization**:
   - Define custom IP ranges and CIDR blocks.
   - Segment networks into subnets.
2. **Isolation**:
   - Keep resources private or expose them to the internet as needed.
3. **Security**:
   - Control traffic using security groups, network ACLs (Access Control Lists), and route tables.
4. **Scalability**:
   - Easily expand or interconnect VPCs as your application grows.

Default vs. Custom VPC

1. **Default VPC**:
   - Automatically created in each AWS region.
   - Includes public subnets and internet access by default.
2. **Custom VPC**:
   - Fully configurable to meet specific needs, such as private networks or hybrid setups.

Subnets, Route Tables, and Security Groups

1. Subnets

A **subnet** is a segment of a VPC where resources like EC2 instances are launched. Subnets are associated with a specific Availability Zone (AZ).

- **Public Subnets**:
  - Subnets with internet access through an Internet Gateway (IGW).
  - Example: Hosting web servers accessible to users.
- **Private Subnets**:
  - Subnets without direct internet access.
  - Example: Hosting databases or backend services.

2. Route Tables

Route tables define how traffic flows within and outside the VPC.

- **Main Route Table**:
  - Associated with all subnets by default unless explicitly overridden.
- **Custom Route Table**:

o   Define specific routes for subnets, such as sending internet-bound traffic to an Internet Gateway.

Example Route Entries:

- Local VPC traffic: 10.0.0.0/16 -> local.
- Internet traffic: 0.0.0.0/0 -> Internet Gateway.

3. Security Groups

A **security group** acts as a virtual firewall for your AWS resources.

- **Inbound Rules**:
    o   Define allowed traffic into the resource.
    o   Example: Allow HTTP (port 80) and SSH (port 22).
- **Outbound Rules**:
    o   Define allowed traffic leaving the resource.
    o   Example: Allow all outbound traffic by default.

4. Network ACLs (Access Control Lists)

- Operate at the subnet level, providing stateless traffic control.
- Allow or deny specific IP ranges for both inbound and outbound traffic.

Setting Up Secure and Scalable Network Architectures

1. Secure Networking

1. **Use Private Subnets**:
    o   Place sensitive resources (e.g., databases) in private subnets to prevent direct internet access.

2. **Enable Network Address Translation (NAT)**:
    o   Use a **NAT Gateway** to allow resources in private subnets to access the internet for updates without being exposed.

3. **Implement Security Groups**:
    o   Restrict access to only necessary ports and IPs.
    o   Example: Allow SSH traffic only from specific IP addresses.

4. **Monitor Traffic**:
    o   Use **VPC Flow Logs** to capture information about IP traffic going to and from network interfaces.

2. Scalable Networking

1. **Elastic Load Balancer (ELB)**:

- o Distribute incoming traffic across multiple instances in public subnets.
- o Use in conjunction with Auto Scaling groups for dynamic scaling.

2. **Multi-AZ Deployment**:
   - o Spread resources across multiple Availability Zones to ensure high availability.

3. **Multi-Region Deployment**:
   - o Deploy resources in multiple regions to serve global users with low latency.

4. **Direct Connect**:
   - o Use AWS Direct Connect for dedicated network connections between on-premises infrastructure and AWS.

Real-World Example: Deploying a Multi-Region Application

Scenario

A global e-commerce platform wants to deploy a multi-region application to:

1. Serve customers across North America, Europe, and Asia.

2. Ensure high availability and low latency.

3. Secure sensitive customer data.

Solution

1. **VPC Design**:
   - Create VPCs in three AWS regions: **US East (N. Virginia)**, **EU (Frankfurt)**, and **APAC (Singapore)**.
   - Define CIDR ranges to prevent overlap (e.g., 10.0.0.0/16, 10.1.0.0/16, 10.2.0.0/16).

2. **Subnet Configuration**:
   - Each VPC includes:
     - Public Subnets: For web servers (e.g., EC2 instances).
     - Private Subnets: For databases and backend services (e.g., RDS).

3. **Routing**:
   - Attach an **Internet Gateway (IGW)** to public subnets for customer-facing traffic.
   - Use **NAT Gateways** for private subnets.

4. **Load Balancing and Scaling**:

- Deploy an **Application Load Balancer (ALB)** in each region to handle incoming traffic.
- Use **Auto Scaling groups** to adjust the number of EC2 instances based on demand.

5. **Database Replication**:
   - Use Amazon RDS with **multi-region replication** to synchronize customer data across regions.

6. **DNS Configuration**:
   - Use **Amazon Route 53** for a global DNS setup:
     - Create a latency-based routing policy to direct users to the nearest region.

7. **Security Measures**:
   - Configure **security groups** to allow only HTTPS traffic on port 443.
   - Enable **VPC Flow Logs** for monitoring and troubleshooting.

Outcome

- Customers experience low-latency access to the application due to region-based deployments.

- High availability is ensured through multi-AZ setups in each region.
- Customer data remains secure and synchronized globally using RDS replication.

Networking is a fundamental aspect of cloud architecture, and AWS VPC provides the flexibility and control needed to build secure, scalable networks. In this chapter, you learned:

1. The basics of VPC, subnets, route tables, and security groups.
2. How to design secure and scalable network architectures.
3. A real-world example of deploying a multi-region application for global reach and reliability.

In the next chapter, we'll explore **Load Balancing and Auto Scaling**, which are crucial for handling traffic fluctuations and maintaining application performance. Let's keep building!

CHAPTER 8: LOAD BALANCING AND AUTO SCALING

Efficient traffic management and dynamic scaling are crucial for maintaining application performance under varying workloads. AWS provides **Elastic Load Balancers (ELB)** and **Auto Scaling groups** to help you build resilient, high-performing architectures. This chapter explains how to use ELB for traffic distribution, Auto Scaling for resource optimization, and monitoring tools to fine-tune scaling policies. Finally, we'll walk through a real-world example of scaling an e-commerce application during sales events.

Using Elastic Load Balancers (ELB) to Distribute Traffic

What is an Elastic Load Balancer (ELB)?

An **Elastic Load Balancer** automatically distributes incoming traffic across multiple targets, such as EC2 instances, containers, or IP addresses, within one or more Availability Zones. It ensures fault tolerance, scalability, and improved application performance.

Types of Elastic Load Balancers

1. **Application Load Balancer (ALB)**:
   o Operates at the **application layer (Layer 7)**.
   o Routes requests based on content (e.g., URLs, headers).
   o Best for microservices and HTTP/HTTPS applications.
2. **Network Load Balancer (NLB)**:
   o Operates at the **transport layer (Layer 4)**.
   o Handles millions of requests per second with low latency.

o   Best for TCP/UDP applications.

3. **Classic Load Balancer (CLB)**:

   o   Operates at both Layer 4 and Layer 7.

   o   Legacy option; newer applications should use ALB or NLB.

Setting Up an Elastic Load Balancer

Step 1: Create an ELB

1. Navigate to the **EC2 Dashboard** and select **Load Balancers**.
2. Click **Create Load Balancer** and choose a type (e.g., ALB).
3. Configure basic settings:

   o   Name the load balancer.

   o   Choose the scheme (internet-facing or internal).

   o   Select listeners (e.g., HTTP or HTTPS).

Step 2: Configure Target Groups

1. Define a **target group** for routing traffic to backend instances.
2. Select a target type:

   o   Instances (EC2), IP addresses, or Lambda functions.

3. Configure health checks to monitor instance availability.

Step 3: Register Targets

1. Add EC2 instances or other targets to the target group.
2. Ensure the targets are in the same VPC as the load balancer.

Step 4: Test the Load Balancer

1. Access the load balancer's DNS name.
2. Verify that traffic is distributed among the registered targets.

Benefits of ELB

- **High Availability**: Distributes traffic across multiple Availability Zones.
- **Fault Tolerance**: Removes unhealthy instances from the traffic pool.
- **Scalability**: Supports dynamic scaling based on workload demands.

Auto Scaling Groups for Handling Varying Workloads

What is Auto Scaling?

An **Auto Scaling group** (ASG) automatically adjusts the number of EC2 instances to match the demand, ensuring cost efficiency and consistent performance.

Key Features

1. **Dynamic Scaling**:
   - Automatically adjusts the number of instances based on predefined metrics (e.g., CPU usage).

2. **Scheduled Scaling**:
   - Adds or removes instances at specific times (e.g., during expected traffic spikes).

3. **Predictive Scaling**:
   - Uses machine learning to forecast and prepare for traffic patterns.

Setting Up an Auto Scaling Group

Step 1: Launch Template

1. Create a launch template with EC2 instance configuration:
   - AMI, instance type, key pair, security groups.

Step 2: Create the Auto Scaling Group

1. Navigate to the **Auto Scaling Groups** section in the EC2 Dashboard.
2. Configure the group:
    o Associate the launch template.
    o Define the VPC and subnets for the instances.
3. Set desired, minimum, and maximum instance counts.

Step 3: Define Scaling Policies

1. Choose scaling strategies:
    o Target Tracking: Scale based on a target metric (e.g., keep CPU usage at 50%).
    o Step Scaling: Add/remove instances incrementally based on thresholds.
    o Scheduled Scaling: Add/remove instances at specific times.

Step 4: Monitor and Test

1. Use **CloudWatch Alarms** to monitor metrics and trigger scaling.
2. Simulate traffic to test scaling behavior.

Monitoring and Tuning Scaling Policies

Tools for Monitoring

1. **CloudWatch Metrics**:
   - Monitor instance health, CPU usage, memory, and network traffic.
2. **CloudWatch Alarms**:
   - Trigger actions when metrics cross thresholds (e.g., high CPU utilization).
3. **AWS Auto Scaling Dashboard**:
   - View scaling history and evaluate policy effectiveness.

Best Practices for Tuning Scaling Policies

1. **Set Realistic Thresholds**:
   - Avoid overly sensitive policies that result in frequent scaling.
2. **Leverage Cooldowns**:
   - Use cooldown periods to stabilize instance scaling after a trigger.
3. **Test with Traffic Simulations**:

- o Use tools like **Apache JMeter** or AWS testing services to simulate workloads.
4. **Combine Scaling Types**:
   - o Use dynamic scaling for unexpected traffic and scheduled scaling for predictable peaks.

Real-World Example: Scaling an E-Commerce Application During Sales Events

Scenario

A popular e-commerce platform anticipates high traffic during its annual sales event. The company needs to:

1. Handle sudden traffic surges without downtime.
2. Maintain a seamless shopping experience.
3. Optimize costs by scaling down after the event.

Solution

1. **Set Up ELB**:
   - o Deploy an **Application Load Balancer (ALB)** to distribute traffic across multiple EC2 instances.

- Use HTTPS listeners to ensure secure customer connections.

2. **Configure Auto Scaling**:
   - Create an Auto Scaling group with:
     - Desired Capacity: 4 instances.
     - Minimum Capacity: 2 instances (off-peak hours).
     - Maximum Capacity: 20 instances (during traffic spikes).
   - Define a target tracking scaling policy:
     - Scale up when CPU usage exceeds 60%.
     - Scale down when CPU usage falls below 30%.

3. **Scheduled Scaling**:
   - Add 10 additional instances at 6:00 AM (start of the sales event).
   - Remove extra instances at 11:00 PM.

4. **Monitoring**:
   - Use CloudWatch to monitor:
     - Request counts per target.
     - Average response times.

- Health checks for instances.

- The platform handles a 10x increase in traffic with zero downtime.
- Auto Scaling ensures optimal performance by dynamically adding or removing resources.
- The company saves costs by scaling down during off-peak hours.

Load balancing and auto scaling are vital for managing application performance, availability, and costs in the cloud. In this chapter, you learned:

1. How to use Elastic Load Balancers (ELB) to distribute traffic.
2. How Auto Scaling groups dynamically adjust resources to handle varying workloads.
3. The importance of monitoring and tuning scaling policies.
4. A real-world example of scaling an e-commerce platform during a high-traffic sales event.

In the next chapter, we'll explore **Cloud Monitoring and Logging**, focusing on tools like CloudWatch and CloudTrail to maintain visibility into your AWS environment. Let's continue building resilient applications!

CHAPTER 9: MANAGING ACCESS AND PERMISSIONS

Access and permissions management is critical for maintaining security and operational efficiency in AWS environments. AWS Identity and Access Management (IAM) is the cornerstone of access control, allowing you to define who can access your AWS resources and what actions they can perform. In this chapter, we'll introduce IAM, cover how to create roles, policies, and users, discuss best practices for managing access in multi-team environments, and walk through a real-world example of granting developers access to specific resources.

Introduction to IAM (Identity and Access Management)

What is IAM?

AWS **Identity and Access Management (IAM)** enables secure control over access to AWS services and resources. With IAM, you can:

1. Create and manage AWS users and groups.

2. Assign permissions using policies.

3. Enable secure resource sharing and automation using roles.

Key Components of IAM

1. **Users**:
   - Represent individuals or services accessing AWS resources.
   - Can have long-term credentials (username and password, access keys).

2. **Groups**:
   - Collections of IAM users.
   - Simplifies permissions management by assigning policies to the group instead of individual users.

3. **Roles**:
   - Assignable identities that AWS services or users can assume.
   - Do not require long-term credentials.
   - Example: Allow an EC2 instance to read data from S3.

4. **Policies**:

- Define permissions for users, groups, or roles.
- Written in JSON format.
- Example: Granting s3:ListBucket and s3:GetObject permissions.

Creating Roles, Policies, and Users

Step 1: Creating an IAM User

1. Go to the **IAM Dashboard** in the AWS Console.
2. Click **Users > Add User**.
3. Enter the user name and select the access type:
   - **Programmatic Access**: For API/CLI usage.
   - **AWS Management Console Access**: For web console access.
4. Attach policies to assign permissions:
   - **Attach existing policies directly** (e.g., AdministratorAccess).
   - **Add the user to a group** with assigned policies.

Example: Create a user developer_user with AmazonS3ReadOnlyAccess.

Step 2: Creating an IAM Role

Roles are used for temporary access or granting permissions to AWS services.

1. Go to **IAM Dashboard > Roles > Create Role**.
2. Select a trusted entity:
   o AWS Service (e.g., EC2, Lambda).
   o Another AWS account.
3. Attach policies to the role.
4. Provide a name (e.g., S3AccessRole) and save.

Example: Create a role for an EC2 instance to read files from an S3 bucket.

Step 3: Writing IAM Policies

IAM policies define the specific actions a user, group, or role can perform.

Policy Example: Read-Only Access to S3 Bucket:

json

{

```
"Version": "2012-10-17",
"Statement": [
  {
    "Effect": "Allow",
    "Action": [
      "s3:ListBucket",
      "s3:GetObject"
    ],
    "Resource": [
      "arn:aws:s3:::example-bucket",
      "arn:aws:s3:::example-bucket/*"
    ]
  }
]
}
```

1. **Effect**: Allow or Deny.
2. **Action**: Specific operations (e.g., s3:ListBucket).
3. **Resource**: Specifies which resources the policy applies to.

Step 4: Attaching Policies

1. Attach the policy to a user, group, or role.

2. Test permissions using the **IAM Policy Simulator** to verify actions allowed by the policy.

Best Practices for Managing Access in Multi-Team Environments

1. **Principle of Least Privilege**:
   o Grant users only the permissions they need to perform their tasks.

2. **Use Groups for Permissions**:
   o Create groups like Developers, Admins, and Support, and assign appropriate policies.

3. **Enable Multi-Factor Authentication (MFA)**:
   o Require MFA for all users, especially those with privileged access.

4. **Rotate Access Keys Regularly**:
   o For programmatic access, ensure that API keys are rotated periodically.

5. **Use Roles for AWS Services**:
   o Assign IAM roles to resources like EC2 instances instead of embedding access keys.

6. **Monitor and Audit Access**:
   - o Enable **CloudTrail** to log IAM activities.
   - o Use **Access Analyzer** to detect over-permissive policies.
7. **Organize Resources with Tags**:
   - o Use tags to identify resources and apply permissions based on tags.
8. **Limit Root Account Use**:
   - o Only use the root account for critical tasks and secure it with MFA.

Real-World Example: Granting Developer Access to Specific AWS Resources

Scenario

A development team is working on a new web application hosted on EC2. They need access to:

1. View logs stored in a specific S3 bucket.
2. Launch and manage EC2 instances in a development environment.

The team should not have access to production resources or administrative privileges.

Solution

1. **Create a Development Group**:
   - Name: DevTeam.
   - Permissions:
     - AmazonEC2FullAccess: Manage EC2 instances.
     - Custom S3 policy for read-only access to the logs bucket.

S3 Policy Example:

json

```
{
  "Version": "2012-10-17",
  "Statement": [
    {
      "Effect": "Allow",
      "Action": [
```

```
    "s3:ListBucket",
    "s3:GetObject"
  ],
  "Resource": [
    "arn:aws:s3:::dev-logs-bucket",
    "arn:aws:s3:::dev-logs-bucket/*"
  ]
 }
 ]
}
```

2. **Add Developers to the Group**:
   - Assign users (e.g., john.doe, jane.smith) to the DevTeam group.

3. **Create IAM Roles for EC2**:
   - Define an IAM role that allows EC2 instances to access the dev-logs-bucket.
   - Attach the role to EC2 instances launched by the development team.

4. **Enable Monitoring**:

- o Use **CloudTrail** to log access activities for both users and resources.

Outcome

- Developers can launch EC2 instances and access logs in the S3 bucket without overstepping into production environments.
- The organization ensures security by enforcing the principle of least privilege.
- Activities are logged and auditable for compliance.

Managing access and permissions is a cornerstone of AWS security. In this chapter, you learned:

1. The basics of IAM, including users, roles, and policies.
2. How to create and assign roles and policies to control access.
3. Best practices for managing permissions in multi-team environments.

4. A real-world example of granting developers access to specific resources while maintaining security and compliance.

In the next chapter, we'll explore **Cloud Monitoring and Logging**, where you'll learn how to track and optimize your AWS environment using tools like CloudWatch and CloudTrail. Let's continue securing and optimizing!

CHAPTER 10: CLOUD MONITORING AND LOGGING

Effective monitoring and logging are essential for maintaining the health, security, and performance of your cloud applications. AWS offers robust tools like **CloudWatch** and **CloudTrail** to help you track metrics, monitor system health, and audit activities. In this chapter, we'll discuss the importance of monitoring in the cloud, explore how to use CloudWatch for metrics and alerts, understand logging with CloudTrail, and apply these tools in a real-world example of debugging performance issues in a microservices architecture.

Importance of Monitoring in the Cloud

Why Monitor Cloud Applications?

1. **Proactive Issue Detection**:
   - Identify problems (e.g., high CPU usage, network latency) before they impact end users.
2. **Optimized Resource Utilization**:
   - Monitor usage to ensure resources aren't underutilized or over-provisioned.
3. **Cost Control**:
   - Detect and address over-provisioned resources to save costs.
4. **Improved Security**:
   - Track unauthorized access attempts or unusual activities.
5. **Compliance and Auditing**:
   - Maintain logs and records to meet regulatory requirements.

Challenges Without Monitoring

- Delayed response to outages or performance bottlenecks.

- Difficulty identifying the root cause of issues.
- Increased costs due to inefficient resource allocation.
- Greater risk of security breaches and data loss.

Using CloudWatch for Metrics and Alerts

What is CloudWatch?

Amazon CloudWatch is a monitoring and observability service that provides:

- **Metrics**: Track performance data for AWS resources and custom applications.
- **Logs**: Collect and store logs for analysis.
- **Alarms**: Trigger notifications or automated actions based on predefined conditions.
- **Dashboards**: Visualize data in real-time.

CloudWatch Metrics

CloudWatch automatically collects metrics for AWS services like EC2, RDS, and Lambda. You can also publish custom metrics.

Common Metrics:

- **EC2**: CPU utilization, disk I/O, network traffic.
- **RDS**: Read/write latency, free storage space.
- **S3**: Bucket size, request count.

Custom Metric Example:

- Track the number of active users in an application:

python

```python
import boto3

cloudwatch = boto3.client('cloudwatch')

cloudwatch.put_metric_data(
    Namespace='CustomAppMetrics',
    MetricData=[
        {
            'MetricName': 'ActiveUsers',
            'Value': 120,
            'Unit': 'Count'
        }
```

```
          ]
     )
```

CloudWatch Alarms

Alarms notify you or take automated actions when a metric breaches
a threshold.

Steps to Create an Alarm:

1. Go to the **CloudWatch Console**.
2. Select **Alarms > Create Alarm**.
3. Choose a metric (e.g., EC2 CPU utilization).
4. Define thresholds:
    o Example: Trigger an alarm if CPU utilization
      exceeds 80%.
5. Configure actions:
    o Send notifications via SNS (Simple Notification
      Service).
    o Auto-scale instances.

CloudWatch Dashboards

Dashboards provide a visual representation of metrics.

Steps to Create a Dashboard:

1. Go to the **Dashboards** section in CloudWatch.
2. Click **Create Dashboard**.
3. Add widgets for metrics (e.g., graphs, gauges).
4. Customize layout and save.

Logging with CloudTrail for Auditing

What is CloudTrail?

AWS CloudTrail records all API activity in your AWS account, enabling auditing and troubleshooting. It logs actions taken via the AWS Console, SDKs, and CLI.

Key Features

1. **Event History**:
   - View the last 90 days of account activity.
   - Identify who made changes to resources and when.
2. **Trails**:
   - Configure trails to store event logs in an S3 bucket for long-term analysis.

3. **Insights**:
    o Detect unusual activity patterns (e.g., excessive API calls).

CloudTrail Setup

1. Navigate to the **CloudTrail Console**.
2. Click **Create Trail**.
3. Configure:
    o Name: audit-trail.
    o Storage: Choose an S3 bucket to store logs.
4. Enable **Management Events** to track API actions.

Analyzing CloudTrail Logs

- **Console**: Use the event history to search by time, resource, or event name.
- **Athena**: Query logs in S3 using SQL for deeper analysis.

Athena Query Example:

sql

```
SELECT eventName, userIdentity.username, sourceIPAddress
FROM cloudtrail_logs
WHERE eventName = 'StartInstances'
```

Real-World Example: Debugging Performance Issues in a Microservices Architecture

Scenario

A company uses a microservices-based architecture for its e-commerce platform. During a high-traffic event, customers experience slow page loads and intermittent errors. The team must identify and resolve the bottleneck quickly.

Solution

1. **Monitor Metrics with CloudWatch**:
   o Use dashboards to track key metrics:
      ▪ EC2 CPU utilization for web servers.
      ▪ DynamoDB read/write capacity units.
      ▪ API Gateway latency.
2. **Set Alarms**:

- o Trigger alarms for:
    - API Gateway latency > 500ms.
    - EC2 CPU utilization > 80%.

3. **Analyze Logs with CloudTrail**:
   - o Check API Gateway logs for failed requests.
   - o Identify unusual spikes in requests to specific microservices.

4. **Investigate Specific Services**:
   - o DynamoDB:
       - Found read capacity units exceeded due to unexpected traffic.
       - Solution: Increase read capacity and enable Auto Scaling.
   - o EC2 Instances:
       - High CPU utilization on instances hosting the checkout service.
       - Solution: Add instances to the Auto Scaling group.

5. **Enable Trace Analysis**:
   - o Use AWS X-Ray to trace requests across microservices.

o   Identify that the bottleneck was caused by a slow payment gateway integration.

Outcome

- The team resolved performance issues by scaling resources dynamically.
- CloudTrail logs provided a detailed audit trail to pinpoint API usage patterns.
- X-Ray traces helped identify and optimize the problematic service.

Monitoring and logging are critical for maintaining application reliability and performance in the cloud. In this chapter, you learned:

1. The importance of monitoring cloud resources.
2. How to use CloudWatch for metrics, alerts, and dashboards.
3. The role of CloudTrail in auditing and security.
4. A real-world example of debugging performance issues in a microservices architecture.

In the next chapter, we'll explore **Backup and Disaster Recovery**, ensuring your data and applications remain resilient in the face of failures. Let's continue building robust cloud systems!

CHAPTER 11: BACKUP AND DISASTER RECOVERY

Data is the lifeblood of modern applications, and ensuring its availability and durability is a critical aspect of cloud architecture. AWS offers a range of tools and services for backups and disaster recovery (DR), allowing organizations to safeguard against data loss and minimize downtime. In this chapter, we'll explore AWS tools like S3, Glacier, and EBS snapshots, learn how to design effective disaster recovery strategies using Recovery Time Objective (RTO) and Recovery Point Objective (RPO), and examine a real-world example of ensuring data durability for a financial application.

AWS Tools for Backups

1. Amazon S3 (Simple Storage Service)
Amazon S3 is ideal for storing backups due to its durability, scalability, and cost-effectiveness.

Key Features:

- **Versioning**:
  - Keep multiple versions of objects to protect against accidental overwrites or deletions.
- **Lifecycle Policies**:

- o Automate the movement of data to lower-cost storage classes or deletion after a specified time.
- **Storage Classes**:
  - o Use **S3 Standard** for frequently accessed backups and **S3 Glacier** for long-term archival.

Use Case: Backing up website content or application logs.

2. *Amazon S3 Glacier*

Glacier is optimized for long-term archival storage and is significantly cheaper than S3 Standard.

Key Features:

- **Durability**: 99.999999999% (11 nines) durability.
- **Retrieval Options**:
  - o **Expedited**: Access data in 1–5 minutes.
  - o **Standard**: Access data in 3–5 hours.
  - o **Bulk**: Access large datasets in 5–12 hours.

Use Case: Archiving compliance data or regulatory documents.

3. *Amazon EBS Snapshots*

Amazon Elastic Block Store (EBS) snapshots provide incremental backups of EBS volumes used with EC2 instances.

Key Features:

- **Incremental Backups**:
    - Only changes since the last snapshot are saved, reducing storage costs.
- **Automated Snapshots**:
    - Use Amazon Data Lifecycle Manager (DLM) to automate snapshot creation and deletion.
- **Cross-Region Copy**:
    - Copy snapshots to other regions for disaster recovery.

Use Case: Backing up a database server or application storage.

4. AWS Backup

AWS Backup centralizes and automates the backup process for multiple AWS services, including:

- S3
- RDS
- DynamoDB

- EBS
- Aurora

Key Features:

- **Policy-Driven Backups**:
  - Define backup plans and apply them to resources automatically.
- **Cross-Region Backups**:
  - Enable disaster recovery by replicating backups across regions.

Use Case: Managing backups for an entire AWS environment.

Designing Disaster Recovery Strategies (RTO and RPO)

What is Disaster Recovery (DR)?

Disaster Recovery refers to the process of restoring IT systems and data after an outage, ensuring business continuity.

Key Metrics: RTO and RPO

1. **Recovery Time Objective (RTO)**:

- The maximum acceptable downtime for a system or application.
- Example: An e-commerce site may require an RTO of 15 minutes.

2. **Recovery Point Objective (RPO)**:
   - The maximum acceptable data loss measured in time.
   - Example: A financial system may have an RPO of 1 hour, meaning data backups must occur at least every hour.

Disaster Recovery Strategies

1. **Backup and Restore**:
   - Store regular backups in S3 or Glacier.
   - Manually restore systems during a disaster.
   - RTO: Hours, RPO: Minutes to Hours.

2. **Pilot Light**:
   - Maintain critical systems in a minimal running state.
   - Scale up secondary systems when needed.
   - RTO: Minutes to Hours, RPO: Seconds to Minutes.

3. **Warm Standby**:

- Keep a scaled-down version of the production environment running.
- Scale up resources during a disaster.
- RTO: Minutes, RPO: Seconds to Minutes.

4. **Multi-Site Active-Active**:
   - Run fully functional systems in multiple regions.
   - Traffic is distributed across sites.
   - RTO: Seconds, RPO: Zero.

Best Practices for Disaster Recovery

1. **Automate Backups**:
   - Use tools like AWS Backup or Data Lifecycle Manager.

2. **Test Recovery Plans**:
   - Conduct regular DR drills to ensure the plan works as expected.

3. **Use Cross-Region Replication**:
   - Replicate data across regions to ensure availability during regional outages.

4. **Monitor Backups**:

- Use CloudWatch to monitor backup success and failure rates.

Real-World Example: Ensuring Data Durability for a Financial Application

Scenario

A financial institution operates a payment processing system that handles sensitive customer transactions. It needs a disaster recovery plan to:

1. Protect data from accidental deletions and cyberattacks.
2. Ensure minimal downtime during outages.
3. Meet compliance requirements for data retention.

Solution

1. **Primary Data Storage**:
   - Use **Amazon RDS** with automated backups enabled to store transaction data.
   - Store audit logs and reports in **Amazon S3** with versioning and lifecycle policies.
2. **Backup Strategy**:

- Enable **AWS Backup** to create daily backups of:
  - RDS database.
  - DynamoDB tables for session data.
- Store backups in S3 Glacier for long-term archival.

3. **Disaster Recovery Plan**:
   - Implement a **Warm Standby** strategy:
     - Deploy a scaled-down copy of the payment processing system in a secondary AWS region.
     - Use **Amazon Aurora Global Database** to replicate the primary database across regions with sub-second latency.

4. **Testing and Monitoring**:
   - Conduct quarterly DR drills to validate the recovery process.
   - Monitor backup status using AWS Backup reports.

Outcome

- The payment system achieves a **RTO of 15 minutes** and **RPO of 5 minutes**.

- Data is replicated across regions, ensuring availability even during major outages.
- The institution complies with regulatory requirements for data retention and security.

Backup and disaster recovery strategies are essential for ensuring data durability and business continuity in the cloud. In this chapter, you learned:

1. How to use AWS tools like S3, Glacier, EBS snapshots, and AWS Backup for effective backups.
2. The importance of RTO and RPO in designing disaster recovery plans.
3. A real-world example of implementing a robust DR plan for a financial application.

In the next chapter, we'll explore **Content Delivery with CloudFront**, focusing on how to accelerate application performance globally. Let's continue building resilient, high-performing cloud architectures!

CHAPTER 12: CONTENT DELIVERY WITH CLOUDFRONT

Content delivery is a critical component of any application that serves users across the globe. AWS CloudFront, a powerful Content Delivery Network (CDN), enables you to deliver static and dynamic content quickly and securely. In this chapter, you'll learn about CloudFront, how to configure its distributions, caching strategies to improve application performance, and a real-world example of delivering video streaming content globally.

Introduction to CloudFront (Content Delivery Network)

What is a CDN?

A **Content Delivery Network (CDN)** is a globally distributed network of servers designed to deliver content to users with minimal latency. Instead of fetching data from a central server, a CDN caches content closer to the user, reducing load times and bandwidth costs.

What is AWS CloudFront?

Amazon CloudFront is AWS's CDN service that integrates seamlessly with other AWS services, such as S3, EC2, and Lambda. It supports both static and dynamic content delivery.

Key Features:

- **Global Edge Locations**:
  - Over 450 edge locations worldwide ensure low-latency content delivery.
- **Content Caching**:
  - Cache content at edge locations for faster delivery.
- **Security**:
  - Integrates with AWS WAF (Web Application Firewall) and AWS Shield for DDoS protection.
- **Customizability**:

- Supports dynamic content delivery via Lambda@Edge.

Common Use Cases:

- Delivering website assets (images, CSS, JS).
- Streaming video content.
- Accelerating API responses.

Configuring CloudFront Distributions

A **CloudFront distribution** defines how content is delivered to end users. Follow these steps to configure one:

Step 1: Create a CloudFront Distribution

1. **Origin Configuration**:
   - Specify the origin where CloudFront will fetch content.
   - Common origins:
     - **Amazon S3**: For static files like images or HTML.

- **Custom Origin**: For dynamic content on an EC2 instance or on-premise server.

2. **Default Cache Behavior**:
   - Define caching rules, such as allowed HTTP methods (GET, POST, etc.).
   - Configure whether cookies, query strings, or headers are forwarded to the origin.

3. **Viewer Protocol Policy**:
   - Enforce HTTPS for secure communication.

Step 2: Configure Cache Settings

1. **Time-to-Live (TTL)**:
   - Set caching duration for content at edge locations.
   - Default TTL: 24 hours.
   - Adjust TTL based on content update frequency.

2. **Origin Shield** (Optional):
   - Add an extra caching layer to reduce origin load for frequently requested content.

Step 3: Enable Distribution

1. Deploy the distribution.
2. Use the CloudFront-provided **Domain Name** (e.g., d123example.cloudfront.net) to access the cached content.

Step 4: Monitor and Optimize

1. Use **CloudFront Logs**:
   o Enable logging to track distribution performance and usage.
2. Integrate with **AWS CloudWatch**:
   o Monitor cache hit ratios, error rates, and latency metrics.

Caching Strategies and Improving Application Performance

Caching is at the core of CloudFront's performance optimization. By caching content closer to users, you can significantly reduce latency and bandwidth usage.

1. Cache Key Customization

- Customize the cache key to determine what is cached.
- Include or exclude headers, cookies, and query strings.

Example:

- Cache different versions of content based on the Accept-Language header to serve localized content.

2. Cache Invalidation

- Use invalidation requests to clear outdated content from caches.
- Example CLI Command:

bash

```
aws cloudfront create-invalidation --distribution-id EXAMPLEDISTRIBUTION --paths "/index.html"
```

3. Compression

- Enable gzip or Brotli compression to reduce file sizes for assets like HTML, CSS, and JavaScript.
- Configurable in the CloudFront settings.

4. Lambda@Edge

- Extend CloudFront functionality by running serverless code at edge locations.
- Use cases:
  - Personalizing content.
  - URL redirection.
  - Security checks before serving content.

Example:

javascript

```javascript
exports.handler = async (event) => {
    const response = event.Records[0].cf.response;
    response.headers['x-custom-header'] = [{ key: 'X-Custom-Header', value: 'MyValue' }];
    return response;
};
```

Real-World Example: Delivering Video Streaming Content Globally

Scenario

A video streaming platform wants to deliver high-definition (HD) videos to users worldwide. The platform must:

1. Ensure fast and uninterrupted streaming.
2. Optimize bandwidth costs.
3. Provide regional content delivery.

Solution

1. **Origin Setup**:
   o Store video files in **Amazon S3** for durability and scalability.
   o Enable S3 Transfer Acceleration for faster uploads.

2. **CloudFront Distribution**:
   o Create a CloudFront distribution with the S3 bucket as the origin.
   o Configure cache behavior:
     ▪ Set a higher TTL for static videos.
     ▪ Forward query strings for adaptive bitrate streaming (e.g., ?resolution=1080p).

3. **Content Segmentation**:
   - Use **HLS (HTTP Live Streaming)** to break videos into smaller segments.
   - Ensure smooth playback by preloading segments in edge locations.

4. **Regional Restrictions**:
   - Use **Geo-Restrictions** to block access in unauthorized regions:
     - Example: Restrict video playback to North America and Europe.

5. **Monitoring and Optimization**:
   - Track **cache hit ratios** in CloudWatch to identify opportunities for optimization.
   - Use **CloudFront Logs** to analyze traffic patterns.

Outcome

- Videos load quickly, even in remote locations, due to edge caching.
- Regional restrictions ensure compliance with licensing agreements.

- Bandwidth costs are reduced by serving content from CloudFront caches instead of the S3 origin.

AWS CloudFront provides an efficient and secure way to deliver content globally with minimal latency. In this chapter, you learned:

1. What CloudFront is and its role as a Content Delivery Network.
2. How to configure CloudFront distributions for static and dynamic content.
3. Strategies to optimize caching and improve performance.
4. A real-world example of delivering video streaming content globally.

In the next chapter, we'll explore **Database Security Basics**, focusing on protecting your data in the cloud with AWS services like IAM, encryption, and auditing. Let's continue building secure and scalable solutions!

CHAPTER 13: BUILDING SECURE APPLICATIONS

Security is paramount when building applications on AWS. AWS employs a **shared responsibility model**, meaning AWS handles the security of the cloud infrastructure, while customers are responsible for securing their applications and data within the cloud. In this chapter, you'll learn about the shared responsibility model, how to implement security best practices across AWS services, and see a real-world example of preventing SQL injection attacks using the AWS Web Application Firewall (WAF).

The Shared Responsibility Model for Security in AWS

What is the Shared Responsibility Model?

The **shared responsibility model** divides security responsibilities between AWS and the customer:

1. **AWS's Responsibility**:
   - o Securing the underlying cloud infrastructure:
     - Physical data centers.
     - Network infrastructure.
     - Host operating systems.
2. **Customer's Responsibility**:
   - o Securing what is built on AWS:

- Applications, workloads, and services.
- Identity and access management.
- Data protection and encryption.

Examples of Responsibilities

Responsibility	AWS's Role	Customer's Role
Data Protection	Secures the physical infrastructure	Encrypts data at rest and in transit
Access Management	Manages AWS root credentials	Configures IAM roles, users, and MFA
Networking	Provides secure network isolation	Sets up VPCs, firewalls, and security groups
Patching	Updates AWS-managed services	Patches OS and applications on EC2

Implementing Security Best Practices Across AWS Services

1. Identity and Access Management (IAM)

- **Use Least Privilege**:
    - Grant only the permissions needed for a specific task.
- **Enable Multi-Factor Authentication (MFA)**:
    - Require MFA for sensitive roles and accounts.
- **Use IAM Roles for AWS Services**:
    - Assign roles to resources like EC2 instead of embedding credentials.

2. Network Security

- **Use Security Groups and Network ACLs**:
    - Allow traffic only from specific IPs and ports.
- **Enable VPC Flow Logs**:
    - Capture and monitor traffic going in and out of your VPC.
- **Deploy Bastion Hosts**:
    - Use bastion hosts for secure SSH/RDP access to private instances.

3. Data Encryption

- **Encrypt Data at Rest**:

- o Use AWS Key Management Service (KMS) to encrypt S3, RDS, and EBS.
- **Encrypt Data in Transit**:
  - o Use SSL/TLS for communication between services.

4. Application Security

- **Implement Input Validation**:
  - o Prevent injection attacks by sanitizing and validating user inputs.
- **Use WAF and Shield**:
  - o Protect applications from common vulnerabilities like SQL injection and cross-site scripting (XSS).

5. Logging and Monitoring

- **Enable CloudTrail**:
  - o Audit API calls and user activity.
- **Monitor with CloudWatch**:
  - o Set up alarms for unusual activity (e.g., failed login attempts).
- **Use AWS Config**:

o Ensure compliance by tracking configuration changes.

6. Regular Security Audits

- **Conduct Penetration Testing**:
  o Simulate attacks to identify vulnerabilities.
- **Use AWS Security Hub**:
  o Get a centralized view of security findings across your AWS environment.

Real-World Example: Preventing SQL Injection Attacks Using AWS WAF

Scenario

A company operates a web application that accepts user input to query a backend database. They discover a vulnerability that allows attackers to execute malicious SQL commands (SQL injection). The goal is to block these attacks while minimizing changes to the application code.

Solution: Deploy AWS WAF

AWS Web Application Firewall (WAF) helps protect applications from SQL injection, XSS, and other common vulnerabilities.

1. **Set Up AWS WAF**:
   - Navigate to the **WAF Console** and create a Web ACL (Access Control List).
   - Associate the Web ACL with the application's **CloudFront distribution** or **Application Load Balancer**.

2. **Enable Managed Rules**:
   - Add AWS-managed rule groups to detect and block SQL injection attempts:
     - Example: **AWSManagedRulesSQLiRuleSet**.

3. **Add Custom Rules** (Optional):
   - Define specific patterns to block or allow traffic.
   - Example: Block requests containing suspicious query strings:

   json

   {

```json
"Name": "BlockSQLInjection",
"Priority": 1,
"Statement": {
  "ByteMatchStatement": {
    "FieldToMatch": {
      "QueryString": {}
    },
    "PositionalConstraint": "CONTAINS",
    "SearchString": "UNION SELECT"
  }
},
"Action": {
  "Block": {}
}
}
```

4. **Monitor and Test**:

   o   Use the WAF **Logs** to monitor blocked requests.

   o   Test by simulating SQL injection attempts:

- Example attack URL:
  https://example.com/products?id=1%20UNI
  ON%20SELECT%20*%20FROM%20users.

5. **Integrate with AWS Shield (Optional):**
   - Protect against DDoS attacks by enabling **AWS Shield Standard.**

Outcome

- The web application blocks SQL injection attempts automatically.
- WAF logs provide visibility into attack patterns, allowing further refinement of security rules.
- The company strengthens its security posture without modifying the application code.

Building secure applications in AWS requires a combination of best practices, proactive monitoring, and the use of AWS tools like IAM, WAF, and CloudTrail. In this chapter, you learned:

1. The shared responsibility model for security in AWS.

153

2. How to implement security best practices across AWS services.

3. A real-world example of preventing SQL injection attacks using AWS WAF.

In the next chapter, we'll explore **Cost Management in the Cloud**, focusing on optimizing AWS resources to reduce expenses while maintaining performance. Let's continue creating secure and cost-effective solutions!

CHAPTER 14: MANAGING COSTS ON AWS

Cost management is a key concern for businesses operating in the cloud. AWS offers flexible pricing models, powerful cost management tools, and strategies to optimize spending without compromising performance. In this chapter, you'll learn about AWS pricing models and billing structures, explore tools like AWS Cost Explorer, Budgets, and Savings Plans, and see a real-world example of reducing costs for a testing environment using spot instances.

AWS Pricing Models and Billing Structures

Pricing Models

AWS provides multiple pricing models to fit different use cases and budgets:

1. **On-Demand**:
   - Pay for compute or storage by the second or hour without upfront commitment.
   - Ideal for unpredictable workloads or short-term projects.

- Example: Testing a new application feature for a few days.

2. **Reserved Instances**:
   - Commit to a 1- or 3-year term to get discounts of up to 75% compared to on-demand pricing.
   - Suitable for predictable, long-running workloads.
   - Example: Hosting a production database.

3. **Savings Plans**:
   - Flexible discount programs based on a committed usage amount (measured in dollars per hour) for 1 or 3 years.
   - Covers EC2, Fargate, and Lambda usage.
   - More flexible than reserved instances as they apply across instance types and regions.

4. **Spot Instances**:
   - Use spare AWS capacity at a discount of up to 90%.
   - Instances can be interrupted when AWS needs capacity.
   - Best for batch jobs, data analysis, or non-critical workloads.

5. **Free Tier**:

- Provides limited free usage of AWS services for 12 months for new accounts.
- Example: 750 hours per month of t2.micro EC2 instance usage.

Billing Structures

1. **Pay-As-You-Go**:
   - Only pay for the resources you consume, without upfront investment.
2. **Tiered Pricing**:
   - Some services offer volume discounts (e.g., S3 storage gets cheaper as usage increases).
3. **Data Transfer Costs**:
   - Inbound data transfer to AWS is free.
   - Outbound data transfer has costs based on volume and region.
4. **Consolidated Billing**:

o Combine multiple accounts under an AWS Organizations structure for unified billing and volume discounts.

Tools for Cost Management

1. AWS Cost Explorer

- Visualize, analyze, and optimize your AWS spending.
- Key Features:
    o Cost and usage breakdown by service, account, or region.
    o Identify trends and forecast future spending.
- Example Use Case:
    o Identify that S3 storage costs are increasing due to unnecessary data retention.

2. AWS Budgets

- Set custom spending limits and receive alerts when thresholds are exceeded.
- Types of Budgets:

- o **Cost Budgets**: Monitor spending against planned costs.
- o **Usage Budgets**: Track resource usage, such as EC2 hours.
- o **Savings Plans Budgets**: Monitor the usage of reserved commitments.
- Example Use Case:
  - o Receive an email alert when EC2 costs exceed $500 in a month.

3. AWS Savings Plans

- Commit to a minimum level of usage (e.g., $10/hour) for 1 or 3 years.
- Covers:
  - o EC2 instances across instance types and regions.
  - o AWS Lambda and Fargate.

4. AWS Trusted Advisor

- Offers cost optimization recommendations, such as:

- Removing unused resources (e.g., idle EC2 instances).
- Right-sizing instances to match workloads.

5. AWS Instance Scheduler

- Automate turning off resources when not in use, such as shutting down non-production instances during off-hours.
- Example:
  - Schedule test servers to run only from 9 AM to 5 PM, Monday to Friday.

Real-World Example: Reducing Costs for a Testing Environment Using Spot Instances

Scenario

A development team needs a cost-effective solution for running a testing environment. The environment includes several EC2 instances that only need to run during the day. The team also wants to save costs without affecting productivity.

Solution

1. **Use Spot Instances for Testing**:
   - o Replace on-demand instances with spot instances for running test workloads.
   - o Configure **Spot Fleet** to ensure availability by using multiple instance types and Availability Zones.
2. **Automate Instance Scheduling**:
   - o Use **AWS Instance Scheduler** to start instances at 9 AM and stop them at 5 PM.
3. **Monitor and Control Costs**:
   - o Set up a **Cost Budget** to receive alerts if monthly testing costs exceed $200.
4. **Optimize Storage Costs**:
   - o Use **EBS Snapshots** to retain testing data and delete unused snapshots regularly using lifecycle policies.

Implementation Steps

1. **Create a Spot Fleet Request**:
   - o Define multiple EC2 instance types in the fleet request (e.g., t3.medium, m5.large).
   - o Specify a target capacity and let AWS fulfill it with the cheapest available spot instances.

Example JSON Configuration:

json

```json
{
  "SpotFleetRequestConfig": {
    "TargetCapacity": 5,
    "LaunchSpecifications": [
      {
        "InstanceType": "t3.medium",
        "SubnetId": "subnet-0123456789abcdef0"
      },
      {
        "InstanceType": "m5.large",
        "SubnetId": "subnet-0123456789abcdef1"
      }
    ]
  }
}
```

2. **Set Up Instance Scheduler**:

o Use an AWS Lambda function or the Instance Scheduler solution from the AWS Marketplace.

o Configure the schedule to stop instances at 5 PM daily.

3. **Monitor Costs**:

o Use **Cost Explorer** to analyze daily spending.

o Set up a **Budget Alert** for testing costs.

Outcome

- The team reduces EC2 costs by 70% using spot instances.
- Automation ensures instances are only active during working hours, saving additional costs.
- The budget alert prevents unexpected expenses.

Cost management is a critical component of running cloud applications efficiently. In this chapter, you learned:

1. The various AWS pricing models and billing structures.
2. Tools like AWS Cost Explorer, Budgets, and Savings Plans for cost management.

3. A real-world example of reducing costs for a testing environment using spot instances.

In the next chapter, we'll discuss **Hybrid and Multi-Cloud Strategies**, exploring how AWS integrates with on-premises and other cloud platforms to provide flexibility and reliability. Let's continue optimizing and building efficient cloud architectures!

CHAPTER 15: HYBRID CLOUD SOLUTIONS

A hybrid cloud approach combines on-premises infrastructure with cloud resources to provide flexibility, scalability, and resilience. AWS offers tools and services, such as AWS Outposts and Direct Connect, to enable seamless integration between your private data center and the AWS cloud. In this chapter, you'll learn about integrating on-premises infrastructure with AWS, explore AWS

Outposts and hybrid connectivity options, and see a real-world example of expanding a private data center using a hybrid model.

Integrating On-Premises Infrastructure with AWS

What is a Hybrid Cloud?

A **hybrid cloud** allows businesses to run workloads across on-premises infrastructure and the cloud, leveraging the strengths of both environments.

Benefits of a Hybrid Cloud Approach

1. **Flexibility**:
   o Migrate workloads to the cloud at your own pace.
   o Keep sensitive workloads on-premises while leveraging AWS for scalability.
2. **Scalability**:
   o Handle sudden traffic spikes by bursting to the cloud.
3. **Resilience**:
   o Use the cloud as a disaster recovery site for on-premises systems.
4. **Cost Optimization**:

o   Reduce capital expenditures by offloading non-critical workloads to the cloud.

AWS Services for Hybrid Integration

1. **AWS Storage Gateway**:
   o   Extends on-premises storage to the cloud.
   o   Use cases:
       ▪   Backup and archiving.
       ▪   Hybrid storage for applications.

2. **AWS Direct Connect**:
   o   Provides a dedicated, high-speed network connection between on-premises infrastructure and AWS.
   o   Benefits:
       ▪   Lower latency and consistent performance.
       ▪   Reduced data transfer costs compared to internet-based connections.

3. **Amazon ECS Anywhere** and **Amazon EKS Anywhere**:
   o   Run containerized applications on-premises while managing them using AWS.

4. **AWS CloudFormation**:

o   Use infrastructure-as-code to manage hybrid environments.

AWS Outposts and Hybrid Connectivity Options

What is AWS Outposts?

AWS Outposts is a fully managed service that extends AWS infrastructure, APIs, and tools to on-premises data centers. It allows organizations to run AWS services locally while integrating with the global AWS ecosystem.

Key Features of Outposts

1. **Consistent AWS Experience**:
   o   Use the same AWS services (e.g., EC2, S3) on-premises as in the cloud.
2. **Low Latency**:
   o   Run workloads that require low latency, such as industrial automation or video processing.
3. **Hybrid Data Processing**:
   o   Process sensitive data locally while using AWS for storage and analytics.

Connectivity Options for Hybrid Architectures

1. **AWS Direct Connect**:
   o Establish a dedicated network connection between on-premises and AWS.
   o Ideal for data-intensive workloads.

2. **Site-to-Site VPN**:
   o Securely connect on-premises networks to VPCs using IPsec tunnels.
   o Suitable for low-cost, smaller-scale environments.

3. **AWS Transit Gateway**:
   o Simplifies connectivity by acting as a central hub for connecting multiple VPCs and on-premises networks.

4. **Hybrid DNS Resolution**:
   o Use Amazon Route 53 Resolver to integrate DNS resolution between on-premises and AWS environments.

Real-World Example: Expanding a Private Data Center Using a Hybrid Model

Scenario

A retail company operates a private data center for core applications, such as inventory management and point-of-sale systems. As the company grows, its data center reaches capacity, and the IT team wants to extend its infrastructure to AWS to:

1. Handle seasonal traffic spikes.
2. Avoid building a new data center.
3. Ensure disaster recovery.

Solution

1. **Deploy AWS Outposts**:
   o Install AWS Outposts in the company's data center to run local workloads with AWS consistency.
   o Use EC2 instances on Outposts for applications requiring low latency.
2. **Set Up Hybrid Connectivity**:
   o Establish a **Direct Connect** link to connect the on-premises data center with AWS for high-speed and reliable data transfer.
3. **Extend Storage with AWS Storage Gateway**:

- Use the gateway to back up inventory data to **Amazon S3**, reducing storage costs.

4. **Disaster Recovery with AWS**:
   - Configure **Amazon RDS** as a failover database in the AWS cloud.
   - Use AWS Elastic Load Balancing to redirect traffic to cloud-based instances during outages.

5. **Monitor and Automate**:
   - Use **AWS Systems Manager** to monitor both on-premises and cloud infrastructure.
   - Automate provisioning with **AWS CloudFormation**.

Outcome

- The company expands its capacity without building a new data center.
- Seasonal spikes are handled seamlessly by bursting workloads to AWS.
- Disaster recovery ensures minimal downtime, protecting critical operations.

Hybrid cloud solutions offer the best of both worlds, allowing businesses to combine on-premises infrastructure with cloud capabilities. In this chapter, you learned:

1. The benefits of integrating on-premises systems with AWS.
2. How AWS Outposts and connectivity options enable seamless hybrid environments.
3. A real-world example of expanding a private data center using AWS hybrid solutions.

In the next chapter, we'll explore **DevOps in the Cloud**, focusing on tools and practices for automating deployment and managing applications efficiently. Let's continue building flexible, resilient architectures!

CHAPTER 16: BIG DATA PROCESSING

Big data has transformed the way businesses derive insights from their operations, enabling organizations to process vast volumes of data efficiently and effectively. AWS offers a suite of tools tailored for big data processing, such as **Amazon EMR**, **Redshift**, **AWS Glue**, and **Athena**. This chapter introduces these tools, explains how to build a data pipeline using Glue and Athena, and provides a real-world example of analyzing customer purchase trends using Redshift.

Introduction to Big Data Tools

1. Amazon EMR (Elastic MapReduce)

Amazon EMR is a cloud-based big data platform for processing large data sets using popular frameworks like Apache Hadoop, Spark, and Presto.

Key Features:

- Easily set up and scale clusters for distributed computing.

- Support for a wide range of tools, including Hive, Pig, and HBase.
- Cost-effective: Leverage spot instances to reduce costs.

Common Use Cases:

- Log analysis and processing.
- Machine learning on massive datasets.
- Real-time analytics pipelines.

2. *Amazon Redshift*

Amazon Redshift is a fully managed data warehouse designed for large-scale analytics.

Key Features:

- Handles petabyte-scale data warehouses.
- Optimized for SQL-based querying.
- Integrates with BI tools like Tableau, Looker, and Power BI.
- Offers **Redshift Spectrum** for querying data stored in S3.

Common Use Cases:

- Business intelligence and reporting.

- Customer behavior analysis.
- Data aggregation across multiple sources.

3. AWS Glue

AWS Glue is a serverless data integration service that simplifies the process of discovering, preparing, and transforming data.

Key Features:

- **ETL (Extract, Transform, Load)**: Create and schedule ETL jobs for data pipelines.
- **Data Catalog**: Automatically discovers and catalogs metadata for datasets.
- **Integration**: Works seamlessly with S3, Redshift, Athena, and other AWS services.

Common Use Cases:

- Data preparation for analytics.
- Migrating on-premises data to the cloud.
- Cleaning and normalizing unstructured data.

4. Amazon Athena

Amazon Athena is a serverless interactive query service that uses SQL to analyze data directly from S3.

Key Features:

- No infrastructure to manage; pay only for the queries you run.
- Compatible with multiple data formats like JSON, Parquet, and ORC.
- Integrates with the AWS Glue Data Catalog.

Common Use Cases:

- Querying log files.
- Ad-hoc analytics on raw data stored in S3.
- Business intelligence exploration.

Building a Data Pipeline with AWS Glue and Athena

A data pipeline automates the flow of data from ingestion to transformation and analysis. Here's how you can build one using Glue and Athena:

1. Data Ingestion

- **Source**: Raw data, such as logs or transaction records, is uploaded to an S3 bucket.
- **Formats**: Supports JSON, CSV, Parquet, and more.

Example: Upload a CSV file containing customer purchase records:

customer_id,product_id,purchase_date,amount
123,456,2023-01-15,29.99
124,457,2023-01-16,39.99

2. Data Cataloging with Glue

- **Create a Glue Crawler**:
  - Configure the crawler to scan the S3 bucket.
  - Automatically discover schema and metadata.
- **Output**:
  - Glue catalogs the data in a table, which can be queried by Athena or Redshift.

3. Querying with Athena

- **Write SQL Queries**:

o　Use Athena to run ad-hoc queries on the cataloged data.

Example Query: Find the total sales by product:

sql

SELECT product_id, SUM(amount) AS total_sales
FROM customer_purchases
GROUP BY product_id
ORDER BY total_sales DESC;

- **Result**:
　　　o　Athena returns the results directly from S3.

4. Automating the Pipeline

- Schedule the Glue crawler and Athena queries using **AWS Step Functions** or **EventBridge** to automate the pipeline.

Real-World Example: Analyzing Customer Purchase Trends Using Redshift

Scenario

A retail company wants to analyze customer purchase trends to identify top-selling products and seasonal buying patterns. The dataset includes millions of transactions stored in S3.

Solution

1. **Data Loading**:
   - Use **AWS Glue** to clean and transform the raw transaction data.
   - Load the transformed data into an **Amazon Redshift** cluster using the **COPY command**.

   Example COPY Command:

   sql

   ```
   COPY customer_purchases
   FROM 's3://retail-data-bucket/transactions/'
   IAM_ROLE
   'arn:aws:iam::123456789012:role/MyRedshiftRole'
   FORMAT AS CSV;
   ```

2. **Data Analysis**:

- o Run SQL queries in Redshift to analyze trends.
- o Example Query: Identify top-selling products by region:

sql

```
SELECT region, product_id, SUM(amount) AS
total_sales
FROM customer_purchases
GROUP BY region, product_id
ORDER BY total_sales DESC
LIMIT 10;
```

3. **Visualize Insights**:
   - o Connect Redshift to a BI tool like Tableau or Power BI to create dashboards.
   - o Example: A heatmap showing sales by product category across regions.
4. **Optimize Performance**:
   - o Use Redshift Spectrum to query historical data directly from S3 without importing it into Redshift.

Outcome

- The company identifies top-performing products and regions, enabling targeted marketing campaigns.
- Seasonal trends highlight opportunities to adjust inventory ahead of peak sales periods.
- The scalable pipeline handles millions of transactions efficiently, reducing manual intervention.

Big data processing is crucial for deriving actionable insights from large datasets. In this chapter, you learned:

1. About AWS tools like EMR, Redshift, Glue, and Athena for big data processing.
2. How to build a scalable data pipeline using Glue and Athena.
3. A real-world example of analyzing customer purchase trends with Redshift.

In the next chapter, we'll explore **Machine Learning on AWS**, showcasing how services like SageMaker enable developers to build and deploy machine learning models. Let's continue building intelligent and data-driven applications!

CHAPTER 17: ARTIFICIAL INTELLIGENCE AND MACHINE LEARNING

Artificial Intelligence (AI) and Machine Learning (ML) are transforming industries by enabling applications to learn, predict, and improve over time. AWS offers a comprehensive suite of AI/ML services, such as **SageMaker**, **Rekognition**, **Polly**, and **Translate**, to simplify and accelerate these capabilities. In this chapter, you'll gain an overview of these services, learn how to train and deploy ML models using SageMaker, and explore a real-world example of building a customer sentiment analysis system.

Overview of AI/ML Services on AWS

1. Amazon SageMaker

Amazon SageMaker is a fully managed service for building, training, and deploying machine learning models.

Key Features:

- **Built-in Algorithms**:
  - Pre-built models for common use cases like regression, classification, and anomaly detection.
- **Training and Tuning**:
  - Simplifies training at scale with managed infrastructure and hyperparameter tuning.
- **Model Deployment**:
  - Deploy models to endpoints for real-time or batch inference.

Common Use Cases:

- Predictive analytics (e.g., sales forecasts).
- Fraud detection in financial transactions.
- Image recognition and classification.

2. *Amazon Rekognition*

Amazon Rekognition provides image and video analysis capabilities.

Key Features:

- Detect objects, scenes, and faces in images or videos.
- Identify celebrities and perform facial analysis.
- Analyze video content for inappropriate scenes.

Common Use Cases:

- Security and surveillance.
- Content moderation for social media platforms.

3. *Amazon Polly*

Amazon Polly converts text into lifelike speech using deep learning.

Key Features:

- Supports multiple languages and accents.
- Custom Voice: Create unique voice profiles.
- Real-time and batch processing.

Common Use Cases:

- Text-to-speech for accessibility tools.
- Automated call center responses.

4. Amazon Translate

Amazon Translate is a neural machine translation service that provides real-time and batch translations.

Key Features:

- Supports over 70 languages.
- Customizable translation for domain-specific language.

Common Use Cases:

- Localizing websites and applications.
- Real-time chat translation for global audiences.

Training and Deploying ML Models in SageMaker

Step 1: Data Preparation

1. **Ingest and Store Data**:
   o Use **Amazon S3** to store training data.
   o Example: A CSV file containing customer reviews with labels indicating sentiment (positive, negative).

2. **Data Cleaning and Transformation**:
   o Use **SageMaker Processing** to clean and preprocess the data.
   o Example: Remove stop words, tokenize text, and encode labels.

Step 2: Model Training

1. **Choose a Built-In Algorithm**:

- Select an algorithm suitable for the problem (e.g., XGBoost for sentiment analysis).

2. **Create a Training Job**:
   - Define the training script and specify input/output locations in S3.
   - Example Python Code:

```python
from sagemaker import get_execution_role
from sagemaker.estimator import Estimator

role = get_execution_role()

estimator = Estimator(
    image_uri='382416733822.dkr.ecr.us-east-1.amazonaws.com/xgboost:latest',
    role=role,
    instance_count=1,
    instance_type='ml.m5.large',
    output_path='s3://my-bucket/output/'
```

```
)
```

```
estimator.fit({'train': 's3://my-bucket/train/'})
```

Step 3: Model Deployment

1. **Create an Endpoint**:
   - Deploy the trained model to a SageMaker endpoint for real-time inference.
2. **Invoke the Endpoint**:
   - Use the AWS SDK to send test data to the endpoint and receive predictions.

Example Python Code:

python

```python
import boto3

runtime = boto3.client('runtime.sagemaker')
response = runtime.invoke_endpoint(
    EndpointName='sentiment-analysis-endpoint',
```

```
    ContentType='text/csv',
    Body='I love this product!'
)
```

```
print(response['Body'].read().decode('utf-8'))
```

Step 4: Monitor and Optimize

1. Use **SageMaker Model Monitor** to track model performance over time.
2. Apply **Hyperparameter Tuning** to improve accuracy.

Real-World Example: Creating a Customer Sentiment Analysis System

Scenario

An e-commerce company wants to analyze customer feedback to understand product sentiment and improve customer satisfaction.

Solution

1. **Data Collection**:
   o Collect customer reviews and ratings from the website and store them in **Amazon S3**.

2. **Data Preprocessing**:
   o Use SageMaker Processing to:
     - Remove HTML tags and special characters.
     - Tokenize and vectorize the text data.
     - Label reviews based on ratings (e.g., 1–2 stars as negative, 4–5 stars as positive).

3. **Model Training**:
   o Use the built-in **BlazingText** algorithm in SageMaker for text classification.
   o Train the model on labeled review data.

4. **Model Deployment**:
   o Deploy the trained model to a SageMaker endpoint.
   o Use the endpoint to predict the sentiment of new reviews in real-time.

5. **Integration**:

- o Integrate the endpoint with the company's analytics dashboard.
- o Visualize sentiment trends over time.
6. **Enhancement**:
   - o Combine results with **Amazon Translate** to analyze reviews in multiple languages.

Outcome

- The company identifies common customer pain points and high-performing products based on sentiment analysis.
- Real-time feedback enables faster resolution of customer issues.
- Multilingual support expands insights into global markets.

AWS's AI/ML services simplify the process of building and deploying intelligent applications. In this chapter, you learned:

1. An overview of services like SageMaker, Rekognition, Polly, and Translate.
2. How to train and deploy ML models using SageMaker.

3. A real-world example of creating a customer sentiment analysis system.

In the next chapter, we'll explore **Internet of Things (IoT) on AWS**, focusing on how to build and manage IoT solutions using AWS IoT Core and related services. Let's continue building innovative cloud solutions!

CHAPTER 18: DEVOPS AND CONTINUOUS DEPLOYMENT

DevOps is a cultural and technical movement that emphasizes collaboration between development and operations teams to deliver applications quickly, reliably, and efficiently. AWS provides a suite of tools to support DevOps practices, including **CodePipeline**, **CodeBuild**, and **CodeDeploy**. In this chapter, you'll learn how to use these tools for DevOps, automate deployments using **Infrastructure as Code (IaC)** with **CloudFormation**, and see a real-world example of implementing CI/CD for a mobile app.

Using AWS Tools for DevOps

1. AWS CodePipeline

AWS CodePipeline automates the end-to-end software release process.

Key Features:

- Supports multiple stages: Build, Test, Deploy.
- Integrates with third-party tools like Jenkins, GitHub, and Bitbucket.
- Automatically triggers workflows based on code changes.

Example Use Case:

- Build a pipeline to deploy updates to a web application hosted on EC2.

2. AWS CodeBuild

AWS CodeBuild is a fully managed build service that compiles code, runs tests, and produces deployable artifacts.

Key Features:

- Scales automatically to handle multiple builds.
- Supports custom build environments using Docker.

- Generates build logs for troubleshooting.

Example Use Case:

- Compile a React app and run unit tests as part of a CI/CD pipeline.

3. AWS CodeDeploy

AWS CodeDeploy automates the deployment of applications to various environments, including EC2, Lambda, and on-premises servers.

Key Features:

- **Blue/Green Deployments**:
  - Deploy to a new environment while keeping the current one live.
- **Rolling Deployments**:
  - Gradually update instances to minimize downtime.
- Tracks deployment success and automatically rolls back on failures.

Example Use Case:

- Deploy a new version of a microservice to a Kubernetes cluster.

Automating Deployments with Infrastructure as Code (IaC)

What is Infrastructure as Code?

Infrastructure as Code (IaC) is a practice of managing and provisioning infrastructure using code rather than manual processes. AWS **CloudFormation** enables you to define AWS resources in declarative templates.

Benefits of IaC

1. **Consistency**:
   o Infrastructure is provisioned exactly as defined in the templates.
2. **Version Control**:
   o Templates can be stored and managed in version control systems like Git.
3. **Automation**:
   o Entire environments can be created, updated, or deleted with minimal manual intervention.

Using AWS CloudFormation

1. **Create a Template**:
   - Define resources like EC2 instances, S3 buckets, and VPCs.
   - Example YAML Template:

   yaml

   ```yaml
   Resources:
     MyBucket:
       Type: "AWS::S3::Bucket"
   ```

2. **Deploy the Stack**:
   - Use the AWS CLI or Management Console to create a stack from the template:

   bash

   ```bash
   aws cloudformation create-stack --stack-name MyAppStack --template-body file://template.yaml
   ```

3. **Update and Manage**:

- Modify the template to add new resources or update configurations.
- Use update-stack to apply changes.

Real-World Example: Implementing CI/CD for a Mobile App

Scenario

A startup is developing a mobile application with frequent updates. They want to implement a CI/CD pipeline to:

1. Automate builds and tests.
2. Deploy the app to a staging environment for review.
3. Release the app to production with minimal downtime.

Solution

1. **Source Control**:
   - Use **CodePipeline** to integrate with a GitHub repository that hosts the app's source code.
2. **Build Stage**:
   - Use **CodeBuild** to compile the app and run unit tests.
   - Define a buildspec.yml file for CodeBuild:

196

yaml

```yaml
version: 0.2
phases:
  install:
    commands:
      - npm install
  build:
    commands:
      - npm run build
  post_build:
    commands:
      - echo "Build completed"
artifacts:
  files:
    - '**/*'
```

3. **Test Stage**:
   o Add a testing phase in CodePipeline to run integration tests using a custom CodeBuild project or a third-party testing service.

4. **Deployment Stage**:
   - o Use **CodeDeploy** to deploy the app:
     - **Staging Environment**:
       - Deploy to an EC2 instance or Elastic Beanstalk environment for internal testing.
     - **Production Environment**:
       - Use **Blue/Green Deployment** to minimize downtime.
5. **Monitoring**:
   - o Use **CloudWatch Alarms** to monitor deployment metrics (e.g., error rates).
   - o Configure automatic rollback in case of deployment failures.

Pipeline Overview

1. **Source Stage**:
   - o Trigger pipeline on GitHub commits.
2. **Build Stage**:
   - o Compile code and run tests in CodeBuild.
3. **Test Stage**:

  o Deploy to staging and validate functionality.

4. **Deploy Stage**:

  o Use CodeDeploy for production deployment.

Outcome

- Developers push updates to GitHub, and the pipeline automatically builds, tests, and deploys the app.
- Blue/Green Deployment ensures minimal disruption during updates.
- Automated tests catch issues early, improving application quality.

AWS provides a rich ecosystem of tools for implementing DevOps and continuous deployment. In this chapter, you learned:

1. How to use AWS tools like CodePipeline, CodeBuild, and CodeDeploy to automate the CI/CD process.
2. The importance of Infrastructure as Code (IaC) using CloudFormation.
3. A real-world example of implementing CI/CD for a mobile application.

In the next chapter, we'll explore **Cost Management for DevOps**, focusing on optimizing CI/CD pipelines and managing infrastructure costs effectively. Let's keep building agile and efficient development workflows!

CHAPTER 19: CONTAINERS AND KUBERNETES

Containers have become the backbone of modern application development, enabling consistent environments for deploying, managing, and scaling workloads. AWS provides two powerful services, **Amazon Elastic Container Service (ECS)** and **Elastic**

Kubernetes Service (EKS), for running containerized applications. In this chapter, you'll learn about these services, how to manage containerized workloads, and explore a real-world example of deploying a scalable microservices architecture using ECS.

Using Amazon ECS and EKS

1. Amazon Elastic Container Service (ECS)

Amazon ECS is a fully managed container orchestration service that simplifies running containerized workloads.

Key Features:

- **Task Definition**:
  - Define how containers should run, including CPU, memory, and networking.
- **Cluster Management**:
  - Automatically manages clusters of EC2 or Fargate instances.
- **Integration**:
  - Works seamlessly with other AWS services like IAM, CloudWatch, and Elastic Load Balancer.

Deployment Options:

- **Fargate Launch Type**:
  - Serverless mode where AWS manages the infrastructure.
- **EC2 Launch Type**:
  - You manage the EC2 instances running the containers.

Common Use Cases:

- Running stateless web applications.
- Batch processing jobs.

2. Amazon Elastic Kubernetes Service (EKS)

Amazon EKS is a fully managed Kubernetes service that allows you to run Kubernetes clusters on AWS.

Key Features:

- **Managed Control Plane**:
  - AWS handles the Kubernetes control plane (e.g., API server, etcd) for high availability.

- **Seamless Kubernetes Experience**:
  - Use standard Kubernetes tools like kubectl and Helm charts.
- **Integration**:
  - Works with AWS services like VPC, IAM, and CloudWatch.

Common Use Cases:

- Managing microservices architectures.
- Migrating on-premises Kubernetes workloads to AWS.

Managing Containerized Workloads

1. Defining Containers

1. **Container Images**:
   - Store your application in Docker images.
   - Push images to **Amazon Elastic Container Registry (ECR)**:

     bash

```
aws ecr create-repository --repository-name my-app

docker      tag      my-app:latest      <account-
id>.dkr.ecr.<region>.amazonaws.com/my-app

docker             push             <account-
id>.dkr.ecr.<region>.amazonaws.com/my-app
```

2. **Task Definition (ECS)**:
   o Specify the container image, resource limits, and networking.
   o Example JSON:

   json

```json
{
  "family": "my-app",
  "containerDefinitions": [
    {
      "name": "web",
      "image": "my-app:latest",
      "memory": 512,
      "cpu": 256
    }
```

```
        ]
    }
```

3. Kubernetes Manifest (EKS):

- o Define workloads using YAML files.
- o Example Deployment:

yaml

```yaml
apiVersion: apps/v1
kind: Deployment
metadata:
  name: web
spec:
  replicas: 3
  selector:
    matchLabels:
      app: web
  template:
    metadata:
      labels:
        app: web
```

```
spec:
  containers:
  - name: web
    image: my-app:latest
    ports:
    - containerPort: 80
```

2. Deploying Containers

- **ECS Deployment**:
  - Use the AWS Management Console, CLI, or CloudFormation to deploy services.
  - Example CLI Command:

  bash

  ```
  aws ecs create-service --cluster my-cluster --service-name web-service --task-definition my-app
  ```

- **EKS Deployment**:
  - Use kubectl to apply Kubernetes manifests.
  - Example Command:

```bash
bash
```

```bash
kubectl apply -f deployment.yaml
```

3. Scaling Workloads

1. **ECS**:
   - Use Auto Scaling to adjust the number of tasks based on metrics like CPU usage.
   - Example Scaling Policy:

   ```bash
   bash
   ```

   ```bash
   aws application-autoscaling put-scaling-policy --service-namespace ecs ...
   ```

2. **EKS**:
   - Scale pods dynamically with the Kubernetes Horizontal Pod Autoscaler.
   - Example Command:

   ```bash
   bash
   ```

```
kubectl autoscale deployment web --cpu-percent=50
--min=2 --max=10
```

4. Monitoring and Logging

- **CloudWatch**:
    - o Use to monitor ECS and EKS metrics like CPU, memory, and task counts.
- **Amazon CloudTrail**:
    - o Track API calls for ECS and EKS for auditing purposes.
- **Container Logs**:
    - o Forward logs to CloudWatch or third-party tools like Splunk.

Real-World Example: Deploying a Scalable Microservices Architecture Using ECS

Scenario

A growing e-commerce platform needs to deploy a scalable architecture to handle its microservices, including:

1. Product catalog service.
2. User authentication service.
3. Order processing service.

The architecture must:

- Handle traffic spikes during sales events.
- Minimize downtime during deployments.
- Support multiple environments (staging and production).

Solution

1. **Set Up ECS Cluster**:
   o Use **AWS Fargate** for a serverless experience.
   o Define task definitions for each microservice.
2. **Configure Load Balancer**:

- Use an **Application Load Balancer (ALB)** to route requests to the appropriate microservices based on URL paths:
  - /products → Product Catalog Service.
  - /auth → User Authentication Service.

3. **Deploy Microservices**:
   - Create ECS services for each microservice.
   - Deploy images from ECR to ECS using task definitions.

4. **Scale Dynamically**:
   - Set up Auto Scaling policies for ECS services:
     - Scale the product catalog service when CPU usage exceeds 70%.
     - Maintain a minimum of 2 tasks for fault tolerance.

5. **Monitor Metrics**:
   - Use CloudWatch to monitor service health and logs.
   - Configure alarms to notify the team of errors or performance issues.

6. **CI/CD Pipeline**:

- o Use **CodePipeline** to automate builds and deployments:
  - Trigger deployments on code commits.
  - Test services in staging before production releases.

Outcome

- The e-commerce platform scales seamlessly during traffic spikes, ensuring no service disruptions.
- Fargate eliminates the need to manage infrastructure, reducing operational overhead.
- CI/CD pipeline accelerates feature delivery while maintaining high reliability.

AWS makes managing containerized workloads easy and scalable with services like ECS and EKS. In this chapter, you learned:

1. The key features and use cases of ECS and EKS.

2. How to manage and scale containerized workloads on AWS.

3. A real-world example of deploying a scalable microservices architecture using ECS.

In the next chapter, we'll explore **Serverless Architectures**, focusing on how AWS Lambda and related services enable fully serverless applications. Let's continue building efficient, modern cloud solutions!

CHAPTER 20: IOT WITH AWS

The Internet of Things (IoT) connects physical devices to the internet, enabling them to communicate, share data, and perform automated actions. AWS IoT Core and its ecosystem of services make it easier to build, deploy, and manage IoT applications. This chapter introduces AWS IoT Core and related services, explains how to build IoT applications for device communication and data analysis, and provides a real-world example of monitoring energy usage with IoT sensors.

Overview of AWS IoT Core and Related Services

1. AWS IoT Core

AWS IoT Core is a managed service that enables secure device communication and data processing for IoT applications.

Key Features:

- **Device Communication**:
    - Supports MQTT, HTTPS, and WebSocket protocols.

- o Devices can publish and subscribe to messages via **IoT topics**.
- **Device Management**:
  - o Maintain and update fleets of IoT devices.
- **Security**:
  - o Use certificates and policies to authenticate devices.

Common Use Cases:

- Smart home devices.
- Industrial monitoring systems.

2. Related AWS IoT Services

1. **AWS IoT Device Management**:
   - o Manage IoT device fleets at scale.
   - o Update firmware and monitor device health.
2. **AWS IoT Analytics**:
   - o Process, store, and analyze IoT data.
   - o Ideal for deriving insights from sensor data.
3. **AWS IoT Greengrass**:
   - o Extend AWS services to edge devices.

o   Enables local data processing and machine learning.

4. **AWS IoT Events**:

   o   Detect and respond to changes in device behavior.

5. **AWS Lambda**:

   o   Trigger serverless actions in response to IoT events.

Building IoT Applications for Device Communication and Data Analysis

Step 1: Connect IoT Devices

1. **Provision Devices**:

   o   Register devices in IoT Core and assign unique certificates for authentication.

   o   Example CLI Command:

   bash

   aws iot create-thing --thing-name EnergySensor001

2. **Set Up Communication**:

- o Use MQTT or HTTPS for device communication.
- o Example MQTT Topic:
  - energy/usage/updates for publishing energy usage data.
  - energy/alerts for receiving alerts from the cloud.

Step 2: Define IoT Rules

1. **Create Rules**:
   - o Use **IoT Rules Engine** to route incoming data to other AWS services like S3, DynamoDB, or Lambda.
   - o Example Rule:
     - Store energy usage data in an S3 bucket:

       sql

       SELECT * FROM 'energy/usage/updates'

       Action: Save data to S3.

2. **Trigger Actions**:

   o   Trigger a Lambda function for real-time processing or alerts.

Step 3: Analyze IoT Data

1. **Data Storage**:

   o   Store raw IoT data in **Amazon S3** or **Amazon DynamoDB**.

2. **Data Processing**:

   o   Use **AWS IoT Analytics** for data cleaning and transformation.

   o   Run SQL queries or train machine learning models on the processed data.

3. **Visualization**:

   o   Connect data to **Amazon QuickSight** for creating dashboards.

Step 4: Manage Devices at Scale

1. **Use IoT Device Management**:

- o Organize devices into groups for easier monitoring and updates.
- o Apply bulk updates to device firmware.
2. **Monitor Device Health**:
    - o Use **CloudWatch** metrics and logs to track device connectivity and errors.

Real-World Example: Monitoring Energy Usage with IoT Sensors

Scenario

An energy company wants to monitor electricity usage in residential homes using IoT sensors. The system should:

1. Collect real-time usage data from smart meters.
2. Alert users when consumption exceeds certain thresholds.
3. Provide analytics for monthly energy reports.

Solution

1. **Set Up IoT Devices**:
    - o Install smart meters in homes to measure energy usage.

o Configure each meter to publish data to the topic energy/usage/updates every minute.

2. **Data Routing**:

   o Use an IoT rule to store incoming data in a DynamoDB table:

   sql

   SELECT * FROM 'energy/usage/updates'

   Action: Save to DynamoDB.

3. **Real-Time Alerts**:

   o Set up another rule to trigger a Lambda function if energy usage exceeds 5 kWh per hour:

   sql

   SELECT * FROM 'energy/usage/updates' WHERE usage > 5

   Action: Publish an alert to energy/alerts.

   o Example Lambda Function:

python

```python
import boto3

def handler(event, context):
    sns = boto3.client('sns')
    sns.publish(
        TopicArn='arn:aws:sns:us-east-1:123456789012:EnergyAlerts',
        Message=f"High energy usage detected: {event['usage']} kWh"
    )
```

4. **Data Analysis**:
   - Use AWS IoT Analytics to process and aggregate daily energy usage for each customer.
   - Store processed data in Amazon S3 for monthly reporting.

5. **Visualization**:
   - Use Amazon QuickSight to generate energy usage dashboards for customers.

Outcome

- Customers receive real-time alerts about high energy usage, helping them conserve energy.
- The company generates detailed reports, providing insights into peak usage times.
- The scalable architecture supports thousands of devices without manual intervention.

IoT with AWS enables businesses to connect devices, process data, and automate actions efficiently. In this chapter, you learned:

1. About AWS IoT Core and related services for managing IoT applications.
2. How to build IoT applications for device communication and data analysis.
3. A real-world example of monitoring energy usage using IoT sensors.

In the next chapter, we'll dive into **Serverless Architectures**, exploring how AWS Lambda and other serverless tools can simplify application development. Let's continue building innovative cloud solutions!

CHAPTER 21: EDGE COMPUTING AND OUTPOSTS

Edge computing brings computation and data storage closer to the location where it is needed, improving response times and saving bandwidth. AWS offers solutions like **AWS Outposts** and **AWS Local Zones** to enable edge computing. In this chapter, you'll learn about edge computing, how to deploy applications closer to users using AWS Outposts, and see a real-world example of running a real-time gaming server at the edge.

Introduction to Edge Computing and AWS Outposts

What is Edge Computing?
Edge computing processes data closer to the source (such as IoT devices, users, or sensors) rather than relying on centralized cloud resources. This reduces latency and ensures faster response times for critical applications.

AWS Solutions for Edge Computing

1. **AWS Outposts**:
   o Fully managed service that extends AWS infrastructure to on-premises locations.
   o Supports the same AWS services, APIs, and tools as the cloud.
2. **AWS Local Zones**:

- Places AWS compute, storage, and networking services closer to users in specific geographic locations.
- Ideal for latency-sensitive applications like video streaming and gaming.

3. **AWS Wavelength**:
   - Integrates AWS services with telecommunications providers to enable 5G edge applications.
   - Best for ultra-low latency workloads like AR/VR or autonomous vehicles.

4. **AWS Greengrass**:
   - Enables edge devices to run AWS Lambda functions and machine learning models locally.
   - Works offline and syncs with the cloud when connectivity is restored.

Why Edge Computing?

1. **Low Latency**:
   - Reduce the round-trip time for data processing.
   - Example: Real-time video analytics.

2. **Bandwidth Optimization**:

- o Process data locally to minimize cloud data transfer.
- o Example: IoT sensor networks.

3. **Regulatory Compliance**:
   - o Keep sensitive data within a specific geographic region.
   - o Example: Healthcare data governed by GDPR.

Deploying Applications Closer to Users for Low-Latency Experiences

1. Using AWS Outposts

AWS Outposts enables running AWS services and workloads locally while maintaining seamless integration with the AWS cloud.

Steps to Deploy Applications Using AWS Outposts:

1. **Order and Install Outposts**:
   - o Choose an Outposts configuration that matches your workload.
   - o AWS delivers and installs the hardware in your data center.

2. **Set Up Networking**:

   o Integrate the Outposts rack with your on-premises network.

   o Use **Direct Connect** or VPN for connectivity to AWS.

3. **Deploy Applications**:

   o Use familiar AWS services like EC2, EBS, and S3 on Outposts.

   o Example: Run a Kubernetes cluster with **EKS Anywhere** on Outposts.

4. **Monitor and Manage**:

   o Use **AWS CloudWatch** and **CloudTrail** to monitor workloads on Outposts.

   o Apply updates and patches seamlessly via the AWS console.

2. Using AWS Local Zones

AWS Local Zones bring AWS services closer to metropolitan areas.

Use Cases:

- Media and entertainment: Render video content locally.
- Gaming: Host multiplayer game servers closer to players.

Deployment Steps:

1. Enable Local Zones in your AWS account.
2. Launch EC2 instances or containers in the Local Zone.
3. Use low-latency networking to connect to users.

3. Combining Edge Computing with AWS Services

1. **Caching with CloudFront**:
   - Use CloudFront edge locations for content delivery.
   - Cache static assets like images, CSS, and videos at the edge.
2. **Edge Processing with Greengrass**:
   - Process IoT data locally and sync results with the cloud.
   - Example: Analyze manufacturing data on factory floor sensors.
3. **Hybrid Workloads with Outposts**:

o Use Outposts for critical on-premises applications while offloading non-critical workloads to AWS cloud.

Real-World Example: Running a Real-Time Gaming Server at the Edge

Scenario

A gaming company wants to provide a seamless multiplayer experience for players around the world. They need:

1. Low-latency game servers to handle real-time interactions.
2. Regional deployment for a consistent experience across geographies.
3. Scalability to handle peak traffic during tournaments.

1. **Deploy Game Servers Using AWS Outposts**:

- Install Outposts in data centers near key gaming regions (e.g., North America, Europe, Asia).
- Run game server applications on EC2 instances on Outposts.

2. **Use Local Zones for Geographic Expansion**:
   - Deploy additional game servers in AWS Local Zones for smaller regions.

3. **Real-Time Data Processing**:
   - Use **Amazon RDS** on Outposts to store player profiles and game stats locally.
   - Sync data with a central AWS S3 bucket for global leaderboards.

4. **Load Balancing and Auto Scaling**:
   - Use **Elastic Load Balancers (ELB)** to distribute player connections across game servers.
   - Enable Auto Scaling to handle traffic spikes during tournaments.

5. **Monitor Performance**:
   - Use **CloudWatch** to monitor server latency and CPU usage.

- o Trigger alarms if latency exceeds acceptable thresholds.

Outcome

- Players experience minimal latency during gameplay, leading to higher satisfaction.
- The architecture scales dynamically during tournaments without manual intervention.
- Regional deployments ensure compliance with data residency requirements.

Edge computing with AWS enables businesses to deliver low-latency, high-performance applications by processing data closer to end users. In this chapter, you learned:

1. About AWS solutions for edge computing, including Outposts and Local Zones.
2. How to deploy applications closer to users for improved performance.

3. A real-world example of running a real-time gaming server at the edge.

In the next chapter, we'll explore **Disaster Recovery and Resilience**, focusing on strategies and tools to ensure business continuity in AWS environments. Let's continue building robust and reliable systems!

CHAPTER 22: SCALING APPLICATIONS GLOBALLY

As businesses grow, scaling applications to serve users worldwide becomes crucial. AWS provides powerful tools for global scalability, such as **Amazon Route 53** for DNS routing and **DynamoDB Global Tables** for multi-region replication. In this chapter, you'll learn how to use these services, implement multi-region architectures, and see a real-world example of launching a SaaS product with users across continents.

Using Route 53 for Domain Management and DNS Routing

What is Amazon Route 53?

Amazon Route 53 is a scalable and highly available domain name system (DNS) service. It helps route user requests to the appropriate endpoints, ensuring low latency and high availability.

Key Features

1. **Domain Registration**:
   - Register and manage domain names directly in Route 53.

2. **DNS Routing**:
   - Translate domain names into IP addresses to direct users to application endpoints.

3. **Health Checks**:
   - Monitor the health of endpoints and route traffic to healthy ones.

4. **Routing Policies**:
   - Choose from various routing strategies to optimize performance and availability.

Common Routing Policies

1. **Simple Routing**:
   - Map a domain to a single endpoint.
   - Example: www.example.com → S3 static website.

2. **Weighted Routing**:
   - Distribute traffic across multiple resources based on defined weights.
   - Example: Gradual rollout of a new application version.

3. **Latency-Based Routing**:
   - Direct users to the region with the lowest latency.
   - Example: North American users routed to US East, Asian users routed to APAC.

4. **Geolocation Routing**:
   - Route traffic based on user location.
   - Example: Direct European users to EU-based servers.

5. **Failover Routing**:
   - Use health checks to route traffic to a backup endpoint if the primary one fails.

Setting Up Route 53

1. **Register a Domain**:
   o Use the Route 53 console to register a domain or import an existing one.

2. **Create a Hosted Zone**:
   o Configure DNS records for the domain.
   o Example: Add an A record to point example.com to an EC2 instance.

3. **Configure Routing Policies**:
   o Use latency-based routing to serve users from the closest region.

Multi-Region Replication with DynamoDB Global Tables

What are DynamoDB Global Tables?

DynamoDB Global Tables provide multi-region, multi-active replication for DynamoDB. This enables applications to serve low-latency reads and writes across multiple regions.

Key Features

1. **Multi-Region Writes**:
   - All replicas in different regions accept read and write operations.
2. **Automatic Conflict Resolution**:
   - Resolves data conflicts based on timestamps.
3. **Seamless Integration**:
   - Works with other AWS services like Lambda and API Gateway.
4. **High Availability**:
   - Ensures data remains accessible even if a region becomes unavailable.

Steps to Set Up DynamoDB Global Tables

1. **Create a DynamoDB Table**:
   - Example Table: Users with attributes UserID, Name, and Region.

2. **Enable Global Tables**:
   - Add replication regions through the DynamoDB console.
   - Example: Replicate the table across us-east-1, eu-west-1, and ap-southeast-1.

3. **Configure Your Application**:
   - Update your application to write to the nearest DynamoDB replica.

4. **Monitor Replication**:
   - Use **CloudWatch** to monitor replication latency and errors.

Best Practices

1. **Optimize Partition Keys**:
   - Ensure a balanced distribution of data across partitions to avoid hot keys.

2. **Use Conditional Writes**:

   o Prevent conflicts by using DynamoDB's conditional write feature.

3. **Monitor Costs**:

   o Multi-region replication can increase costs; monitor usage to optimize.

Real-World Example: Launching a SaaS Product with Users Across Continents

Scenario

A tech startup is launching a SaaS product with users in North America, Europe, and Asia. The application requires:

1. Low-latency performance for all users.
2. High availability across regions.
3. A seamless experience during failover scenarios.

Solution

1. **Domain Management with Route 53**:
   - ○ Register the domain saasproduct.com with Route 53.
   - ○ Configure latency-based routing to direct traffic to the nearest AWS region:
     - ▪ US East (Virginia), EU (Frankfurt), and APAC (Singapore).

2. **Multi-Region DynamoDB Global Tables**:
   - ○ Create a global table UserPreferences to store user settings.
   - ○ Replicate the table across the three regions.

3. **Application Architecture**:
   - ○ Deploy the application backend on **Elastic Beanstalk** in each region.
   - ○ Use **Amazon S3** and **CloudFront** to deliver static assets globally.

4. **Load Balancing and Failover**:
   - ○ Configure **Application Load Balancers (ALBs)** in each region.

- Use Route 53 failover routing to redirect traffic to a backup region during outages.

5. **Monitoring**:

    - Enable **CloudWatch Alarms** to monitor endpoint health and DynamoDB replication latency.

    - Set up **AWS Trusted Advisor** to optimize performance and security.

Outcome

- Users in North America, Europe, and Asia experience fast and reliable service.

- DynamoDB Global Tables ensure consistent data access across regions.

- Failover mechanisms guarantee high availability, even during regional disruptions.

Scaling applications globally requires careful consideration of latency, availability, and data replication. In this chapter, you learned:

1. How to use Route 53 for domain management and global DNS routing.
2. The benefits and setup of DynamoDB Global Tables for multi-region replication.
3. A real-world example of launching a SaaS product to serve users worldwide.

In the next chapter, we'll explore **Cost Optimization for Global Architectures**, focusing on strategies to manage and reduce expenses while maintaining performance at scale. Let's continue building resilient, cost-effective solutions!

CHAPTER 23: THE FUTURE OF CLOUD COMPUTING WITH AWS

The cloud landscape is constantly evolving, with AWS at the forefront of innovation. From emerging trends in AI and quantum computing to sustainability initiatives, understanding where the cloud is heading helps businesses stay competitive and forward-thinking. In this chapter, we'll explore these trends, AWS's green cloud practices, and advancements in serverless computing, capped off with a real-world example of adopting a cloud-first strategy to adapt to the future.

Emerging Trends in AWS Services

1. Machine Learning and AI Evolution
AWS continues to lead in machine learning (ML) and artificial intelligence (AI) innovations:

- **Customizable AI Services**:
    - Amazon SageMaker makes AI accessible to non-experts with features like AutoML and built-in algorithms.

- **Domain-Specific Solutions**:
    - Services like **Amazon HealthLake** cater to healthcare data analytics.
- **Edge AI**:
    - AWS Greengrass enables machine learning on edge devices, reducing reliance on centralized processing.

2. Quantum Computing

Quantum computing is poised to revolutionize problem-solving in areas like cryptography, materials science, and complex optimization.

- **Amazon Braket**:
    - A managed service for quantum computing experiments.
    - Offers access to quantum simulators and real quantum computers.
- **Use Cases**:
    - Financial portfolio optimization.
    - Drug discovery simulations.

3. Serverless and Event-Driven Architectures

The future is serverless, with AWS Lambda continuing to expand its capabilities:

- **Graviton2 Processors**:
  - Lower-cost, energy-efficient processors for serverless environments.
- **Container Support**:
  - Run Docker containers on Lambda for complex workloads.
- **Event-Driven Systems**:
  - Native integration with services like Amazon EventBridge enables scalable workflows.

4. Multi-Cloud and Hybrid Cloud

While AWS is a leader in cloud services, businesses are increasingly adopting hybrid and multi-cloud strategies.

- **AWS Outposts and EKS Anywhere**:
  - Bring AWS infrastructure to on-premises or hybrid setups.
- **Interoperability**:

- Enhanced APIs for integrating with other cloud providers.

Sustainability Initiatives and Green Cloud Practices

AWS is committed to sustainability, with several initiatives aimed at reducing environmental impact:

1. Renewable Energy Goals

- AWS aims to power all operations with 100% renewable energy by 2025.
- Builds solar and wind farms globally to offset energy consumption.

2. Energy-Efficient Infrastructure

- **AWS Graviton Processors**:
  - Custom-designed chips that consume less power and reduce carbon footprints.
- **Cooling Efficiency**:

o Advanced cooling technologies in AWS data centers lower energy usage.

3. Green Software Practices

- Tools like **AWS Compute Optimizer** help customers right-size instances to avoid waste.
- Sustainability dashboards in **AWS Well-Architected Tool** allow businesses to track environmental impact.

Preparing for the Future of Cloud

1. Adopting Quantum Computing

Businesses should start experimenting with quantum algorithms to solve complex problems.

- Use **Amazon Braket** to simulate quantum scenarios.
- Train teams on quantum programming languages like Qiskit.

2. Scaling with Serverless

As serverless computing matures, organizations can:

- Transition monolithic applications to microservices on Lambda.
- Use **Amazon EventBridge** for event-driven workflows.
- Explore hybrid serverless models with **AWS Outposts**.

3. Enhancing Data Sovereignty

With stricter data privacy regulations worldwide:

- Leverage **AWS Local Zones** to keep data within specific regions.
- Adopt encryption tools like **AWS Key Management Service (KMS)** for data protection.

Real-World Example: Adapting to the Future with a Cloud-First Strategy

Scenario

A global logistics company wants to future-proof its IT infrastructure. The goals include:

1. Leveraging emerging cloud technologies.
2. Reducing its carbon footprint.
3. Maintaining agility to adapt to industry changes.

Solution

1. **Quantum Experimentation**:
   o Use **Amazon Braket** to simulate supply chain optimization problems.
   o Explore quantum algorithms for better route planning.
2. **Serverless Adoption**:
   o Migrate internal applications to AWS Lambda.
   o Use **Amazon DynamoDB** for real-time tracking of shipments.
3. **Sustainability Initiatives**:
   o Implement **Compute Optimizer** to identify and eliminate underused resources.
   o Choose Graviton-based EC2 instances for reduced energy consumption.

4. **Multi-Cloud Strategy**:

   o Deploy AWS Outposts in regional warehouses to ensure low-latency operations.

   o Use **Direct Connect** for integration with other cloud platforms.

5. **Data Compliance**:

   o Use **AWS Local Zones** to store data in compliance with regional data privacy laws.

Outcome

- The company reduces operational costs by 20% through serverless adoption.
- Quantum simulations provide a 15% improvement in delivery route efficiency.
- Sustainability goals are achieved by cutting carbon emissions from IT operations by 30%.

The future of cloud computing is shaped by emerging technologies, sustainability, and the push for serverless and hybrid models. In this chapter, you learned:

1. About trends like quantum computing, serverless advancements, and multi-cloud strategies.
2. AWS's sustainability initiatives and green cloud practices.
3. A real-world example of adapting to the future with a cloud-first strategy.

This concludes our journey through **Practical AWS: Cloud Solutions with Real-World Use Cases**. With these insights, you're well-equipped to innovate, optimize, and lead in the evolving cloud landscape. Keep building the future!

www.ingramcontent.com/pod-product-compliance
Lightning Source LLC
LaVergne TN
LVHW051445050326
832903LV00030BD/3245